18 (

From Psychopath to Proselyte

Dan Stevens

outskirts
press

18 and Life
From Psychopath to Proselyte
All Rights Reserved.
Copyright © 2021 Dan Stevens
v3.0 r1.9

The opinions expressed in this manuscript are solely the opinions of the author and do not represent the opinions or thoughts of the publisher. The author has represented and warranted full ownership and/or legal right to publish all the materials in this book.

This book may not be reproduced, transmitted, or stored in whole or in part by any means, including graphic, electronic, or mechanical without the express written consent of the publisher except in the case of brief quotations embodied in critical articles and reviews.

Outskirts Press, Inc.
http://www.outskirtspress.com

Paperback ISBN: 978-1-9772-3670-8
Hardback ISBN: 978-1-9772-3741-5

Cover illustration is property of Dan Stevens, but was created by Nirbheek Ahmed. Realistically, I have no artistic drawing skills of my own. If you wish to use him for illustrating a book, you can contact him at www.fiverr.com, then search for nirbheek. He's a great guy who does good work!

Outskirts Press and the "OP" logo are trademarks belonging to Outskirts Press, Inc.

PRINTED IN THE UNITED STATES OF AMERICA

Table of Contents

1:	The Lawnmower Man	1
2:	Basic Training	17
3:	Rules of Engagement	43
4:	Subdivisions	63
5:	'Hood Life	81
6:	Holy Roller	101
7:	Addicted	116
8:	Hero	127
9:	Crash & Burn	142
10:	Riders on the Storm	155
11:	Youth Gone Wild	168
12:	... on the road to Damascus	182

About the Author	203

The Lawnmower Man

> *"Ricky was a young boy, he had a heart of stone*
> *Lived nine to five and he worked his fingers to the bone*
> *Just barely out of school, came from the edge of town.*
> *Fought like a switchblade so no one could take him down*
> *he had no money, no ... no good at home*
> *walked the streets a soldier, really fought the world alone"*
>
> *"18 and Life"*, Skid Row

Rarely do I meet people whose minds get so warped that they quickly lose all capacity to function in this world, without hating just about everyone and everything. It usually starts small and builds over time, resulting from some form of abuse at home, school or elsewhere. So begins this story of a man like that – I call him Ricky, based on the lyrics of the song I started the chapter with. This story deals with all the negative ways Ricky's childhood upbringing turned him into the borderline psychopath he became as a young adult. My friendship with Ricky began when he started attending school. From there it was an on again / off again friendship that didn't fully develop until Ricky started college. Either way, I was always there for him. As such, I can speak to many of the negative effects his upbringing had on him, having heard Ricky talk about many of them throughout his life.

These psychotic tendencies began shortly after Ricky graduated college, but they had been living inside him his whole life. The challenge with Ricky was his unwillingness to trust others. This distrust was largely a result of Ricky's conclusion that he only knew two types of people growing up: those that abused him, or those that taught him nothing on how to constructively deal with all the pain that he felt from the abuse. As for the source of the abuse, I'll discuss that in more detail in a later chapter. Ricky spent close to two decades suppressing his anger and his quest for revenge towards his abusers. It greatly fueled the growth of the psychotic monster inside of him. He never said anything, his body language said it all. I could easily see who Ricky was becoming. I tried to help, but from his adolescent years onward, even I eventually lost Ricky's trust. Lately, I see an increasing trend where people manifest similar psychopathic behavior more frequently. The many news stories about some depraved student shooting up his fellow students and/or teachers at school, or some young adult shooting random strangers at a mall or concert, are two of the more popular examples. This psychotic behavior is getting more out of hand each day, and the increase in fear it leads society to embrace, is not something I enjoy having to witness.

While at college, Ricky was free from both his parents' protection and his fear of them. The exhilarating feeling of being unshackled from his crippling fear of disobeying his parents, gave Ricky the freedom to experiment with all the activities he was never permitted to try at home. However, this freedom slowly made him more emotionally distant. It was as if he was turning into an entirely different person. It started out innocent at first, taking photographs for the school yearbook and other things like that. Even then he was denied his due, as the editor gave credit for his photos to another volunteer photographer. He tried lots of other free-spirited activities during and after college, like getting stoned with the marijuana smoking fraternity on campus, partying every weekend, or trying to get to know a high school girl whose picture he saw in the local paper just because he could. Once he earned his degree, he was now completely free.

After graduating college, Ricky moved into an off-campus party house known as Looney Tunes. It was an appropriate description of what life was like inside Ricky's head. This freedom eventually led him to do things that most people considered either wrong or unhealthy: a diet consisting of mostly beer, pasta with butter, or snack chips as his three main food groups, stealing food and skimming money from his employers, buying alcohol or cigarettes for minors, burning large stacks of papers in the backyard – which once led to the fire department being called, peeing in the backyard when the one bathroom was being used – while ignoring a neighbor screaming at him as he did, carelessly running up credit card balances without concern for the financial implications involved with not paying them back, to name a few. It was all a fun, liberating, experimental game Ricky liked playing, and he didn't care about the consequences. That boldness is usually the start of an increased desire to manifest more psychotic behavior.

Ricky's roommates at Looney Tunes had recently discovered a brand-new form of entertainment called the Ultimate Fighting

Championship, where their thirst for violence was satisfied on a monthly basis through discovering which form of martial arts was the best way to either knock your opponents out or get them to submit due to pain. Based on where Ricky was headed, he desired more of this entertainment. He eventually found a way to satiate his growing bloodlust, when he discovered a hardcore wrestling organization called Extreme Championship Wrestling (ECW) while visiting his parents that first Christmas after getting his college degree. As I'll mention in a later chapter, Ricky grew up watching the World Wrestling Federation and World Championship Wrestling every week, but as his bloodlust for being entertained through violence matured, WWF and WCW got boring. This new extreme version fully satisfied his bloodlust. Some of the matches consisted of replacing the ring ropes with barbed wire, or anything goes matches, where Ricky got to witness wrestlers being hung by their neck off the side of a production truck with an industrial size chain link tow strap, body slammed through a burning table, hit in the forehead with an aluminum beer can, or hit with kendo sticks and/or other assorted household items used to make people bleed. Ricky's favorite were the trashcan matches with all sorts of improvised weapons placed in the trashcan. It was in one of these matches where he got to see a wrestler, known in wrestling circles as New Jack (RIP), use a stapler to staple an opponent's eyeball. Some of the matches were so gruesome and involved so much blood, most people would wonder how a wrestler survived such a massive blood loss. While those thoughts did occasionally cross Ricky's mind, he didn't have much in the way of conscientious concern for those that entertained him, so long as he was entertained.

It was through ECW that Ricky discovered his new role model. He went by the name Raven. Now Raven had his own unique cryptic style of controlling people as the main heel, or bad guy for those of you not into wrestling. He usually led the less talented misfits who weren't very good wrestlers. They all became better working together as part of his "flock", as influenced by Raven's cryptic psychological leadership style. Because of his past abuse, Ricky took the cryptic mindset Raven used to control the misfits in wrestling, to create the ideal persona he wanted to emulate in his own life. In an interview Raven recently conducted with writer Michael Wonsover, he said this about how he created his wrestler persona: "I created Raven from the five-year old in me who never felt like he got enough love or attention. That's where Raven comes from and part of me – 4 1/2 decades later – is still trying to protect my fragile five-year old self." Raven adds: "I'll be the character that I actually am inside. The tortured soul." According to Wonsover, this 'tortured soul' spawned the character that defined him, Raven – "a narcissistic loner dressed in concert t-shirts, ripped jeans, and a leather jacket. He used the experiences from his damaged childhood as bullets against his opponents while begging for sympathy from fans. The Raven character identified with the ever-changing culture of the 90s" … Raven concludes: "I was able to be in angles where I used psychological warfare, which is always more intriguing than physical warfare. If I wanted to make you mad, I could beat you up. You'd be in pain, but you'd get over it. But if I took your girlfriend, that's an emotional pain and that is so much harder to deal with. I always caused emotional pain and emotional damage to my opponents and most people didn't do that." [1] In addition to his similar desire to inflict emotional pain on people like others did

---

[1] Michael Wonsover, *Raven's Flight Through Wrestling History*, June 6, 2017, ESPN.com. https://www.espn.com/wwe/story/_/id/19561086/raven-recalls-career-journey-spanned-all-three-major-companies-wwe-ecw-wcw-biggest-moment-wrestling-history

to him, Ricky could also relate to hanging around misfits, like Raven's flock, who weren't considered all that important in life. Since his foray into the internet world began shortly after that, the email address Ricky chose reflected this desire to emulate Raven's cryptic personality, so he too could influence others just like Raven did on TV. The email address Ricky used was <u>ravenmod@----.com</u>, with the mod being an acronym for master of deception. I didn't use the actual email address, as someone reading this might consider the idea of sending him death threats. If Ricky were still around, he'd probably be doing the same thing in return. Unfortunately, when he returned to Looney Tunes he couldn't find ECW episodes on cable TV, so he had his mom record each weekly episode and send him the VCR tapes every few weeks.

When Ricky wasn't satiating his thirst for freedom through entertaining bloodlust, he found himself going along with all the other forms of entertainment his roommates often participated in, the more notable ones being watching either Beavis and Butt-Head episodes or listening to the Jerky Boys. For those that have ever heard or watched either, helping a person mature was not the goal of either program. Sure they were entertaining in their own immature way, but they certainly didn't give Ricky any basis for developing a maturity of his own, a maturity he was never given any guidance on how to develop prior to graduating college. He was finally free to develop it after graduating college. I discuss the details why in a later chapter.

Until he got that college degree, Ricky also received no guidance or wisdom when it came to making important life decisions for himself. He did get to experiment with life experiences that allowed him to try new things for himself while at college, to finally learn what was or was not acceptable, but he was never allowed to take control over his dreams and goals in life. Once he had that degree, this light at the end of the tunnel that was complete freedom and independence, shone on him like a scorching midday sun in the middle of a desert. However, once Ricky experienced the heat at the end of the tunnel that accompanied the light, with regards to his maturity, he quickly discovered he had no water to drink.

The musical influences that arose from his desire for freedom and independence weren't helping him mature either. Since the musical style known as grunge rock was popular at that time, the effects of its depressing tone / lyrics also contributed to the psychotic side of Ricky. Though they are not technically considered grunge rock, Ricky's favorite band at that time was Queensrÿche. Their breakout album involved a cryptic storyline that featured a hitman who had a former prostitute turned nun and a Catholic priest as his only acquaintances. The album was called Operation: Mindcrime, which was totally on point, as far as a description of the effects it had on the person Ricky was becoming. Based on what I witnessed, I can say with absolute certainty that Operation: Mindcrime was a huge success for Ricky. Now I am not writing this to advocate for or against the influence of rock music on a person's mental state, but in Ricky's case, he certainly never developed enough maturity to know better.

Because his parents always labelled him a genius, he also got himself heavily involved in reading. He initially got into it as a way of trying to develop his identity as a responsible adult. It also helped him catch up on his attempts to understand himself and his role as an adult in the world he lived in, having received very little guidance from his parents. I will discuss his relationship with his parents in more detail in the next chapter. Having had an abusive and mentorless past, Ricky was what you'd call a late bloomer – intellectually and emotionally. Thanks to influences like Raven and Queensrÿche, along with his abusive past, Ricky found himself easily able to relate to secular philosophers like Kant, Hegel, Descartes, Hume, and his personal favorite – Nietzsche. Unfortunately, as I'm about to describe, instead of helping him mature, it led him further down a dark, sadistic path, far away from any semblance of integrity or compassion for his fellow men and women. Since Ricky was now free to explore life on his own, and with little guidance present at any point in his life, he didn't truly recognize where he was going in life, and honestly, he didn't care.

Philosophically speaking, Kant and Hegel both promoted the idea that moral thought is something humans individually decide for themselves, and that there are no moral absolutes. In his book Beyond Good and Evil, (Ricky's favorite book at the time) Nietzsche took this concept one step further, claiming that a personal desire to rise to power was something that existed beyond the religious concept of moral absolutes, hence the title Beyond Good and Evil. Because of this desired quest for a superior state of being that Nietzsche believed all humans were to pursue for the sake of self, he also implied that it was entirely acceptable for the strong to exercise control over the weak in a healthy society. Since Ricky still wasn't physically strong, all those times where he was told he was mentally strong led him to focus on developing his superior mental state. Which left Ricky to pursue the goals set forth in Operation: Mindcrime, trying to discover what lied Beyond Good and Evil, with the professional wrestler Raven as his ideal cryptic role model, all while being regularly entertained by the most violent or childish forms of entertainment, built on a foundation full of abuse and neglect.

Now it shouldn't be difficult for most anyone to see this as a recipe for disaster. When a person's mental state is unhealthy, it is easy for someone to believe in ones' capacity for achieving a superior state. Thanks to his new secular role models, this was Ricky's time to showcase his superior mental state for the glory of claiming his position of power in the world. The more this toxic concoction continued to brew in his mind, heart and soul, the less he cared about others.

The last chemical in the toxic concoction that was added to Ricky's mind was the title of this chapter. It was a movie based on a Stephen King book that Ricky watched around that time. In the movie an unintelligent country adult named Jobe, from a small town, is often bullied by everyone in this small town. In the midst of his abuse, Jobe catches the eye of a renowned scientist, who chooses Jobe for an experiment to attempt to increase his intelligence. So Jobe undergoes a series of sessions where he is rapidly exposed to information through a virtual computer headset. Within a few months of treatments, Jobe becomes extremely intelligent through virtual information overload, to the point where he has absorbed so much information so quickly, he gains the ability to perform such feats as manipulating matter via telekinesis. Jobe uses those abilities to get revenge against all the people who abused him for his perceived inferiorities. Jobe did so through actions such as stopping a moving bullet coming towards him at full speed using only his mind, then redirecting the bullet back at the shooter at the same speed, or the ability to separate all the individual atoms of a person's body so that the person ceases to exist. There were many other "telekinetic feats" that Jobe did in the movie. To fully understand the plot, I suggest renting the movie. After having seen the movie, this was the final piece in Ricky's quest for personal power, giving him both the opportunity to manifest his lust for vengeance, while helping him recognize his potential to become just like Jobe and develop the superior mental state Nietzsche and others convinced him existed in the realm "beyond good and evil". To use a Biblical analogy, it was as if Ricky became totally obsessed with gorging himself on every last piece of fruit he could get his hands on from the tree of the knowledge of good and evil, to learn what existed beyond it.

As for how that influenced who Ricky was becoming, I will let some of his actions speak for themselves.

"Tequila in his heartbeat, his veins burned gasoline
It kept his motor running, but it never kept him clean
They say he loved adventure, Ricky's the wild one
He married trouble, and had courtship with a gun
Bang bang, shoot 'em up, the party never ends
You can't think of dying when the bottle's your best friend"

"18 and Life", Skid Row

It was another beautiful spring Saturday in the world. Kids were playing little league baseball, parents were enjoying watching their kids learn the competitive aspects of teamwork, pushing themselves to excel at athletic pursuits. It was an idyllic dream – for everyone except Ricky. Ricky was only there because it was his job to ensure all the games had umpires. He didn't really care about anyone else there, so long as he did what he was expected to do and impressed his boss enough to let him keep his job. This one particular Saturday he let his sadistic side influence his decision to have some fun of his own. He took his car keys and stuck them in between his fingers, then approached a kid leaning against a chain link fence with his hand, punching the palm of the kid's hand through the fence with his keys before quickly walking away so as not to be caught in the act and identified as the guilty party. Before he could be identified, Ricky managed to get away. After all, he still had to protect his job, and honesty certainly wasn't going to help him.

One night I was with Ricky as he was driving home, very pissed off at the world. In his rush to get home, he was driving somewhere around 50 mph in a residential zone where the speed limit was only 25 mph. There was a police officer in the area, who pulled Ricky over. When the officer approached, Ricky already had his license and registration ready to give the officer. As the officer tried to introduce himself, Ricky quickly gave the officer what he wanted before he even asked for it. Ricky had obviously been in this position before. As he did, he interrupted the officer, snapping back with a reply of, "Can you just shut the hell up, give me my damn ticket, and let me get the hell out of here?" I especially remembered the words "hell, damn, hell" coming from his mouth, which were entirely appropriate considering who he was becoming, and just how quickly he was heading down that psychotic path to hell, though I still held out hope Ricky wouldn't end up there. When the officer returned, he was polite, trying to calm down this arrogant kid riding a Dodge Omni harder than it was probably meant to be driven. Most cops would have arrested Ricky based on his attitude. In trying to keep the peace, he actually complied with Ricky's demand, and gave him the ticket. As he tried lecturing Ricky to slow down, Ricky merely pretended to comply before leaving for the final leg home.

———◆———

After having lived in the low-income house known as Looney Tunes for some time after college, the ongoing issue of the dishes never getting washed continually ate at Ricky's mind and soul. Because he was raised in a military family where chores were done as a prerequisite for sleeping in the house that night, Ricky was the only one who ever bothered to clean up after himself. It got to the point where Ricky had to secure his own dishes in his room to ensure they remained clean. But with all the other dishes never getting cleaned, Ricky rarely had enough room in the sink to clean his own dishes. So around noon one day Ricky decided to send a message to the slobs in the house who never washed their dishes, by leaving the kitchen sink running for hours. He knew no one else would be home for at least another four hours, so he had plenty of time to get his message across. For the rest of that afternoon, Ricky sat alone in his upstairs room, anger pooling up in his heart at about the same rate that the water pooled on the kitchen floor downstairs. The best way to describe his thought process was to compare it to Private Pyle's mental state, in the bathroom scene from Full Metal Jacket where he kills the drill sergeant, and then himself. With a chef's knife in hand (it was clean by the way, Ricky wasn't a slob who would use a dirty knife), Ricky was ready to defend his actions by any means necessary. When the landlord came home, a fierce yelling match took place. After the anger standoff had ended, Ricky realized he wasn't going to have to defend himself with the knife like he planned. Thinking quickly, he offered the landlord the knife, challenging him to try and kill him instead. The landlord took the knife from Ricky, then whipped it at Ricky's box fan, chipping a fan blade in the process. He then stormed out of the room, leaving Ricky alone in his room to depressurize his anger while analyzing what happened. A few hours later, he finally calmed down enough to head downstairs to make himself a late dinner, without saying anything to anyone.

———◆———

Later on that summer, Ricky did say something to anger a close friend of the group, who everyone simply referred to as shark. In retaliation, the shark took a bite out of Ricky in the form of a hard punch to the ribs. Ricky was never a big fan of sharks – especially not this idiotic, mentally inferior one. After taking that punch that bruised his ribs, and also his pride, the toxic thought process of revenge, similar to the mindset of Private Pyle in the bathroom scene I just described, slowly began to take over Ricky's mind. After a few weeks he sought opportunities to swim alone with each shark – not only the one that hurt him but also the rest of the shiver that defended shark. Having been a baseball player, he figured the best way to deter a future shark attack was to knock out each member of the shiver, via a well-placed sneak attack to either the side of the ribs or the head with a baseball bat, when the opportunity presented itself.

———◆———

All these incidents slowly continued to agitate the toxic

concoction of psychotic behavior inside Ricky's immature, unstable, twisted mind. A good part of each day was consumed by thinking about the many ways he imagined getting back at everyone in his life who had abused him or made him feel like he was worthless. The rope noose he hung from his door only served to remind everyone of what he stood for. Because of all the pain he felt inside, his only real motivation was to discover ways to get others to feel the same emotional pain he often did as a child.

It was the type of thing you might watch in an episode of a made for TV crime drama. Many of them feature a character portrayed as a psychotic monster who likes to torture and abuse others in a secluded part of the world, like an abandoned cabin in a remote area of a forest or wilderness. That idea gave Ricky a location through which to eventually satiate his bloodlust for revenge. It didn't matter how psychotic the thought was or what it cost to carry it out. He only dreamed of showing the world what it felt like to go through everything he had to endure from the day his abuse first started. Hate – and only hate – flowed through his severely depraved mind, an unfortunate result of years of neglect and abuse. Finding victims to torture and entertain his sick mind was a bit more challenging.

Though his physical build was an obstacle to overcome people – deep down he was still a wimpy kid – he sought to figure out ways to utilize his perceived superior mental capacity to take advantage of any limitations his body placed on him. Once he got others trapped in his abandoned, lonely, dark world of misery, his only desire was to get people to feel the pain he often felt. With a heart as cold and black as the dried blood he sought to take from others, finding creative ways to inflict upon others the pain he was forced to relive in his mind consumed him more with each passing day. The most disturbing part was how he once concluded that he was more important than God. This is what happens when unstable people with an abusive past are given the opportunity to push the limits of sanity. Pride and/or revenge are the motivating factors, and Ricky's mind and heart certainly possessed high quantities of both. Until that one fateful morning when that all changed dramatically ...

April 19, 7:45 am

"Hurry, up you idiot. We've got to get the truck in place during normal delivery hours, before all the employees show up. If we don't they might get suspicious."

"Alright, I'm coming already. Quit pestering me!"

"Did you park the escape vehicle where I told you?"

"YES! I parked it exactly where you told me to. Sometimes you can be so damn anal."

"Well if we're going to pull this off, we have to plan everything right. If we don't, our plan of revenge will fail. I DO NOT FAIL! You understand? Revenge is the only option for us."

"What happens if we get caught?"

"Who cares if we get caught! Our job is to send the government an important message, and that's all we are here to do."

"And that message is ... ?"

"To show all the clowns running this government that infringing upon our first and second amendment rights is not to be tolerated. The government does not care about equal rights for all anymore. Ruby Ridge? Branch Davidian compound? Hellllooooooo? They mean anything to you? The system is corrupt and needs to be exposed."

They had planned this for months. All the equipment had been bought. The chemicals were correctly made. The truck was loaded up and ready to move. All systems go!

The events in question happened in Oklahoma City back in 1995, and unfortunately the plans of Timothy McVeigh and Terry Nichols on that now infamous date in history were successful, when they did send a message to the United States government by blowing up the Alfred P. Murrah federal building.

As Ricky sat in front of the TV, mesmerized by the destruction he saw on the morning news, both to the building itself and especially all the dead bodies, he finally saw in himself the possibility of living up to his untapped potential to display the power that existed "beyond good and evil", and on a national scale. But Ricky experienced something unusual that morning, something he was totally unprepared for.

2

Basic Training

> *"I got no face, no name, I'm just a killing machine*
> *I cut the population down, if you know what I mean*
> *I never stop in one place, I move about the cities*
> *Got expensive tastes, but I hasten to add that*
> *I'm the best that there is"*
>
> "Killing Machine", Judas Priest

WHAT MAKES THE GRASS GROW, PRIVATE?

BLOOD! BLOOD MAKES THE GRASS GROW, DRILL SERGEANT!

Molding a soldier into a killing machine is what every drill sergeant lives for. The joy of watching puny, scraggly nobodies become heartless killing machines, now that is a life of honor and prestige! It didn't matter where you came from. The unflinching job of a drill sergeant was to prepare you for the rigors of killing your enemy, physically AND mentally. The mental training the soldier received was as important to their survival as the physical training. In order to kill their enemies, the soldier had to have a heart and mind as cold and black as the steel of their weapon. No one embodied a cold, black heart better than a drill sergeant. Toughness was not just an act for them, it was their whole reason for existence. Being a drill sergeant always meant being the alpha male. It didn't matter who else was in the group. The drill sergeant either became the alpha male or died trying. They always knew how to overcome all physical challenges. No one could stand up to a drill sergeant and expect to win. Rarely did a soldier try. A good example of this heartless drill sergeant would be Gunnery Sgt. Hartman (played by Lee Ermey), from the movie Full Metal Jacket.

In the late 1950's this was the first taste of adulthood experienced by Ricky's dad. Playing high school football prepared Ricky's dad to possess the mindset that allowed him to handle military life in the late 1950's. To hear Ricky describe his dad, he figured his dad's first role model was probably his high school football coach. Only eighteen and fresh out of high school, his second role model – if you can call him that – was his drill sergeant. Any veteran from that era can tell you that U.S. military life was much tougher than it is now. Most drill sergeants would also tell you they don't want to be anyone's role model. Their only purpose was to teach every recruit how to face off against an enemy in a foreign country and heartlessly kill any and all enemies first. The mental and emotional strain involved with fighting a war under survival of the fittest rules can be extremely taxing to both mind and body. Hence the need to train the future soldier in the art of fighting and survival. Only the toughest of the tough were able to make it through training.

Occasionally there was a soldier who thought he was bigger or stronger than a drill sergeant. As a young child, Ricky's dad once told Ricky a story about the time his drill sergeant was challenged to a fight by a fellow recruit in basic training. The fight didn't last very long. This unfortunate recruit learned the hard way just how physically strong and emotionally heartless a drill sergeant was. Once the drill sergeant won the fight by knocking the soldier out cold, he started working over the soldier's face with his fists – forehead, eyes, cheeks, nose, and even the ears. Then he worked his way down to the neck muscles until they were black and blue as well. Then the shoulders. Quadriceps. Triceps. Biceps. Wrists. Hands. Stomach. Pectorals. Delts. Trapezius. Groin. Thighs. Hamstrings. Knees. Calves. Ankles. Feet. If the muscle had a name, this drill sergeant beat it until it bruised. Severely. Once the "fight" was over, you would not have been able to tell what skin color the soldier originally had – it was now a combination of black, blue and purple. For the rest of the recruits, the pain that recruit must have experienced after regaining consciousness, while laid up in a hospital bed, must have left an impact on the rest of the soldiers, Ricky's dad included.

This story was Ricky's most memorable, haunting story he remembered his dad tell growing up. Whether it was a true story or not was something Ricky never knew for sure, but he thought it best to believe it was a true story. To Ricky, this always seemed like more than a story. His dad usually acted like a drill sergeant around Ricky. As a result, growing up inside the walls of his house, Ricky always lived in fear this could one day happen to him.

Ricky's dad was a stocky brute weighing roughly 210 lbs, a 5' 8" tank of a man who repaired heavy, neon billboard signs forty+ hours a week, with a no-nonsense, physically-oriented personality to match. He was often required to lift parts up to the billboard where the sign was located fifteen to twenty feet in the air. At home he lifted barbells for about thirty minutes every day, at least until he retired to his almost nightly ritual of drinking beer while either channel surfing through the different stations to find something worth watching on TV, or reading a sci-fi novel.

His dad was raised in upstate New York, along with his younger brother, Ricky's uncle. They were raised in a family that was half German, one quarter Irish and one quarter Dutch. Along with his physical conditioning, Ricky's dad developed the German temper and the Irish passion for drinking. Ricky never did find out why his dad drank so heavily. In the interest of self-preservation, he never asked. He wanted to, but not if it meant finding out what would happen if his dad chose to do something other than answer him honestly. He certainly remembered all the anger outbursts when his dad drank. It must have been something soldiers did when they weren't out on patrol, Ricky surmised. When Ricky's dad was only fourteen, his mom passed away. He never talked about her, so Ricky didn't know her at all. He never even knew her name. Opening up that possible wound by asking about her wasn't a door Ricky wanted to open either.

After high school Ricky's dad enlisted in the Army. In the 1950's you could go to college, which few did. Those that came from families that couldn't afford to send their kids to college or who weren't smart enough to get accepted, either learned a technical trade skill, or joined the military to perform the lowest, most dangerous tasks such as infantry – the military calls them grunts. Ricky's dad chose the military as a grunt, with a promise from his dad (Ricky's grandfather) that a sponsorship with the International Brotherhood of Electrical Workers (IBEW) awaited him once he completed his military contract.

Shortly after his mom's passing, Ricky's dad moved to the same urban area where Ricky's mom grew up, and they both went to the same high school. Ricky thought it had something to do with his mom's passing away, but he never learned how his dad ended up there or why he moved there either. The only other things he learned about his dad's childhood was that he played football in high school, enjoyed country music and beer, was an Army grunt who served in Korea during the uneasy truce that followed the wartime fighting, made some mean dill pickles, and ... and ... honestly, Ricky didn't know anything else about his dad. Because their bond was based mostly on fear, there was never any open communication. When a bond is based on fear, there rarely ever is.

As a grunt serving in Korea, Ricky's dad endured the typical military training of his day, and though he never saw combat due to serving under an uneasy truce between the US and Korea, he accepted an honorable discharge after his four-year enlistment ended. Since his roles as football player, infantry grunt and/or electrician were the only ones he ever knew, Ricky's dad for the most part raised Ricky to ensure he used his mind instead, so as not to have to live the same life his dad lived. His already decided future as a white-collar executive was totally in opposition to the blue-collar, military style upbringing he was raised with. Beneath the surface, given the strict discipline that ruled the house, while his dad wanted him to live a white-collar life, Ricky only witnessed life from the perspective of a blue-collar redneck soldier fighting a war he knew nothing about. The heroes in this story were soldiers and gladiators, athletes who played the game of professional football. From the time he was six years old, he watched these Giant gladiators in football equipment play football every Sunday afternoon. He also watched his dad drink – a lot – whenever they played. When they won, his dad wasn't as belligerent. When they lost, it was better not to say anything for fear of his dad's drunken outbursts. His dad never hit Ricky, but hearing Ricky recount all those times his dad would scream expletives like a drill sergeant, that haunting story about the drill sergeant beating up that recruit, and all his drunken anger outbursts made Ricky wonder if it was just a matter of time before his dad crossed that line too. Ricky didn't know how else to react but with fear. The mental image of Ricky's dad as that drill sergeant doing to him what his drill sergeant did to this unnamed recruit terrified Ricky. It was not the kind of pain Ricky himself wanted to endure. As a scrawny child, he certainly didn't have the physical build to resist or endure his dad's drill sergeant mentality gone wrong. So he pretended to display courage, when he really didn't have any. A good soldier always does.

"DAAAAD!!!" Ricky yelled from the top of the stairs. "DINNERTIME!"

"I didn't ask you to yell to him from the top of the stairs. I could have done that. Go down there and tell him dinner's ready!", snapped Ricky's mom.

Ahh, the dreaded trip downstairs to get dad to come to the dinner table. On weeknights, dad only had one hour to drink before dinnertime, so he didn't drink too much. Weekends were usually much worse, more so after a Giants loss on Sunday afternoon. Aside from the regular Sunday morning activity, dad had all weekend to sit around and drink. Regardless of the day, all the children feared this daily assignment – even on weekdays. If you can call it an assignment. Nightmare would be more appropriate. Ricky slowly made his way downstairs.

He slowly passed through the door, located to the right side of the foyer, to enter the TV room. Thankfully, Ricky's dad was still in the far corner of the room, sitting in his ugly banana yellow recliner with the curved wooden armrests. Open beer can in one hand, remote in the other, his eyes were glued firmly to the TV.

Ricky timidly interrupted the TV volume, "Mom told me to tell you dinner's ready, dad."

"Tell your mother I'll be up in five minutes. I want to finish this beer."

"OK, dad", said Ricky, quickly sprinting up the stairs on his way back to the kitchen table for dinner, thankful he was able to avoid having to get too close to the monster in the banana recliner.

"Did you tell your father dinner's ready?"

"Yes, mom," said Ricky in between gasps for air, still winded from the sprint as he sat at his assigned seat. "He said he'll be up in five minutes."

The rest of the family sat there painfully enjoying the wonderful smell of the food mom prepared, getting hungrier, forced to wait until dad came before anyone could eat. Five minutes came and went, and still no dad at the dinner table.

"Ricky, go get your father and make him come upstairs for dinner. Tell him I said he needs to come up RIGHT NOW!"

Being a harbinger of bad news is not something a child enjoys. Sharing it with a drunken angry monster almost three times your size makes it even more dangerous. Ricky sighed as he got up from his chair, wondering why he was chosen to face this nightmare again. With shoulders hunched in despair, Ricky hesitated before slowly leaving the kitchen. The dad monster wasn't in view as he left. Dejected, he slowly sauntered towards the stairs a second time. Still no sign of the monster approaching. He paused with another sigh at the top of the stairs, hoping the monster would magically appear through the doorway at the bottom, saving him from the risk of getting too close to the foul, alcoholic breath weapon of the monster lurking downstairs. Ricky paused to let out a third sigh, then used his best stealth skills to quietly tiptoe to the bottom of the stairs. Ricky sighed another quick breath before fearfully turning the corner, quickly, to enter the downstairs dungeon where the drunken, angry monster inhabiting his father's body likely still lurked. Fortunately, he was still sitting in his ugly banana recliner across the room. In situations like this, distance was Ricky's best asset. Ricky let out a sigh of relief.

Timidly entering the monster's lair, Ricky's eyes intently locked onto the monster, just like a mountain lion who spotted his next potential meal.

Despite the small tone of relief in his voice from the distance separating them, Ricky quivered, "Dad, mom told me to tell you she wants you upstairs right now."

"G&* D&*#IT!", screamed Ricky's father in response as he began the process of standing up. "Tell your mother I'm coming already."

"OK, dad," Ricky blurted, not at all concerned whether he was heard as he sprinted back up the stairs to the kitchen, starting his sprint well before his dad even finished standing up. He had witnesses in the kitchen.

As Ricky quickly returned to his seat, he panted, still winded from his successful escape, "Mom, dad said he's on his way."

"OK, Ricky, thanks."

When dad did finally join the family at the dinner table, proper etiquette at the dinner table was expected to be adhered to. It was emphasized so the kids all learned to eat like normal humans did when eating out at restaurants. Such etiquette included holding silverware the right way, and asking for food instead of reaching across the table for it. Anytime one of the kids tried to reach for food without asking for it, dad often tried stabbing the kids with the tines of his fork. Thankfully, Ricky did always manage to be a little quicker than his dad anytime he tried that, and never got stabbed with the fork. That was how Ricky developed his quick reflexes.

A similar rule applied to cleaning dishes after each meal. Whoever was assigned dish detail was expected to thoroughly clean them every night. If they were still dirty after the first wash, they would have to be cleaned again. And again. So there were many nights when each of the children had to remain in front of the kitchen sink until all the dishes were thoroughly washed correctly. It is from this experience that Ricky's dad often gave his wisest bit of advice: "Do the job right the first time, so you don't have to do it over and over again."

"Get off me, you jerk", Ricky snapped, while trying to wrestle free from his brother. "It's my video game and I'm still using it."

"I don't care", replied Ricky's brother, trying to pry the game free from Ricky's feeble attempt at a deathgrip. "You've had it long enough and now I want to play it."

"NO! You're not getting it until I'm done with it. LET GO!"

"NO WAY! I'm going to get that game from you, so I can play

it!", said Ricky's brother, while grappling with Ricky for control of the game.

"HEY, KNOCK IT OFF!", yelled mom to both boys. "What did I tell you boys about fighting?"

Ricky's mom grabbed his brother, attempting to separate them. His brother tried to break free, inadvertently hitting mom in the process. When she recovered, she angrily grabbed both boys using all her strength to ensure neither one got away, one by each arm and gave them a lecture that also haunted Ricky for years.

Mom snapped, "You can beat up each other, or your sister, until you're both black and blue. You can try to beat up your dad if you can. However, if you EVER lay a hand on me like that again, you better sleep with one eye open every night or run away, because I will get even with you, and it won't be pretty." Sadly, this wasn't the only time Ricky would hear her say that.

———◆———

Born to parents that were equal parts Italian, Welsh and Scottish, Ricky's mom lived in a similar low-income neighborhood near their high school. Her parents spent quite a bit of their time growing up in Sicily. Their Italian heritage and traditions heavily influenced Ricky's mom growing up. She also grew up with their religious and family beliefs. I will address the religious aspect more in a later chapter.

Regarding day to day life, Ricky's mom and her brother grew

up where the only opportunities they were afforded to grow socially, were either to play with boys her age, or no one at all. Toughness was not an act for Ricky's mom, it was a necessity. To overcome the challenges she faced in her "survival of the fittest" environment with only boys, she learned to stand up to all the boys her age. She had to – there were no girls her age to develop friendships with. She also got into smoking cigarettes once she was legally able to, as that was part of the persona she believed she had to adopt in order to fit in among all the boys in her neighborhood.

When she graduated high school, her parents enrolled her in secretarial school. Back in the 1950's, there was still a subtle form of gender bias towards men being the ones going to college or pursuing technical trades, while the women stayed home to work, or worked in careers more tailored towards women. Also, Ricky wondered, given how his mom lived in a poor neighborhood, maybe her parents couldn't afford to send her to college. Instead, they felt sending her to secretarial school would be just as beneficial for her future, only not as expensive. Once she graduated, secretarial jobs were very easy to find for women. Career wise, they didn't create any long-term job stability, nor did they pay well, but they helped keep the bills paid.

Though Ricky's mom and dad went to the same high school, they didn't meet and get to know each other until after high school. Ricky remembers it had something to do with a high school related event, but couldn't provide any more details. Again, his parents never shared much about their personal life with Ricky. Once they got married in 1966, they lived in a few places before buying the house that would become the family home in 1969. Ricky only knew that because it was etched into the concrete by the back door of the house. Though married, their lifestyle was the same. Both lived like blue-collar rednecks. Ricky's dad still drank and his mom still smoked cigarettes.

In August of 1970, they learned they were pregnant with their first child. While Ricky knew his dad still drank long after he was born, his mom told him that she quit smoking once she learned she was pregnant with Ricky. Somehow, Ricky believed his mom didn't quit until a few months after she learned she was pregnant. While Ricky can't prove with any certainty exactly when she quit, he believed her pre-natal smoking resulted in him developing two minor deformities in his life. One was physical, the other neuro-biological. Neuro-biologically, for as long as I knew Ricky, he was a perfect fit for someone with Attention Deficit Disorder. In spite of the potential risks from smoking, Ricky's infant years were very helpful for his parents, or so I was told. He hardly ever cried and rarely woke his parents up at night.

Dealing with the challenges that having Attention Deficit Disorder (ADD) posed was often hard for Ricky. Being able to focus was never his strength. Throughout his school years, he occasionally blacked out for as long as ten minutes. Most of the time it occurred at home when he had to get ready for school, but there were other times, which I'll describe later on in Ricky's story, where a blackout manifested itself in the most inopportune times. Thankfully for both him and his parents, he was not hyperactive. I'm sure family life would have been much harder for them all if he was hyperactive too.

Given how his parents were not intellectuals, they did not

know much about medical or social disorders. Many of today's disorders simply didn't exist back in the 1970's. To their blue-collar mindset, Ricky simply lacked focus. The belief that their children had anything wrong with them was a belief they never allowed anyone to accept. Knowing your strengths is important to your development. So is understanding your weaknesses.

As an intellectual, Ricky would have wanted to know everything wrong with him. Unfortunately, knowledge was not something Ricky was taught to discover for himself outside of school. When you grow up in an age where access to information takes hours or days to find, knowledge is not something that comes easily. When you are raised by two blue-collar parents, knowledge isn't actively promoted at home either. However, wanting to be a good soldier in this military squad called a family, Ricky knew he was not allowed to question their authority. A good soldier never does.

Ricky's physical deformity was finally dealt with when he was five years old. The medical term for Ricky's physical deformity was an affliction called monorchism, which according to most websites, occurs in 3-4% of normal males, and 25-30% of prematurely born males. One primary risk factor for monorchism is tobacco consumption by the mother prior to birth, which could also explain the possibility of Ricky being born prematurely. In ordinary terms, monorchism meant Ricky was born with only one testicle. In most cases, premature births instead develop cryptorchidism, where the testicle remains in the abdomen instead of properly descending to the scrotum. In most cases of cryptorchidism, the testicle usually works its way down to its proper location within the first year of life. If it doesn't, surgery is usually required after a year.[2] The doctor did scan for the missing testicle, but never found it. If it did exist and was undescended, but was not treated in the first year of a boy's life, the likelihood of testicular cancer would have been much greater. Ricky's parents did not take care of this until he was five, taking him to a local hospital surgeon to fix it. Thankfully it was monorchism, which meant no testicle, and no likelihood for cancer.

Since Ricky was sedated for the entire surgery, he had no memory of it happening. The trauma involved with the experience is something no five-year old should have to endure. However, the one thing that Ricky did remember from that experience, was the memory of his parents not being there for support. The only person that was there for him was his grandfather from his mom's side, Grandpa John. As a result, Ricky always looked forward to seeing Grandpa John come visit, because he longed for a mentor to guide him, someone that would spend quality time with him and give him the sage advice all children long for, regardless of whether or not they can express it, in all the many ways that his parents never stepped up to provide. John was Ricky's best opportunity for that long-desired mentor.

Ricky also remembers getting a teddy bear before the surgery. For most of his life he thought it came from Grandpa John, only to learn years later that the teddy bear came from his grandfather from his dad's side, Vernet. The intent was to give him something he could keep by his side to remind him that he wasn't alone. Since there was rarely anyone to support him, that little teddy bear ended up being the only continuous source of

---

[2] https://en.wikipedia.org/wiki/Cryptorchidism

support for Ricky – his security blanket, so to speak. Many years later, having endured dozens of stitching repairs, that little teddy bear from his grandfather did more to help him through the painful memories of his childhood than anything else, including his parents. Once he was old enough to understand what his grandfathers did for him, in honor of them, Ricky named the teddy bear J.V., which was short for John Vernet.

"How are you feeling, Ricky?", asked the doctor.

"I'm OK," said Ricky.

"You don't feel any pain in your groin?"

"No. Should I?"

"No. However, now that your surgery is done, I have to ask you an important question."

"OK. What's the question?"

"Do you want me to insert a plastic testicle to replace the one you were born without? It would be very helpful for you to have it."

"No, I think I'm fine like this", Ricky replied, naïvely thinking this option to be less painful, and involve no more surgery. Like most five-year old children, the overall ramifications of big decisions like these are not ones they are able to understand on their own.

"Are you absolutely sure this is what you want?", replied the doctor.

"Yes," said Ricky, displaying some hesitation in his answer to the doctor's question.

"OK, then. I'll send in a nurse in a few minutes to finish up so you can go home", said the doctor with a confused look on his face as he left Ricky there alone in his room.

Based on having been asked a second time, the question slowly gnawed at Ricky's soul as he sat there alone after his surgery. In spite of the distance between him and his parents, he wished one of them would have been there to help him understand the future implications of his decision – implications most five-year-old children don't understand.

Ricky sat there, equally confused at both the doctor's question, and being asked it a second time. With each passing second alone in the room, Ricky kept nervously asking himself, "What if I made the wrong decision? Is this decision as important to my future as the doctor seems to make it to be? Is it too late to change my mind, or am I stuck with this decision forever?"

As Ricky pondered those questions for what seemed like an agonizing eternity, the nurse eventually arrived to finish up with final checkout. By the time she arrived, the anguish involved with his decision screamed inside his soul louder than the music at a rock concert. He wanted to ask her if he could talk to the doctor again, to find out the reasons why the doctor would ask that question twice. He also wanted to ease the screaming inside his soul. On the other hand, he wanted to embody the soldier his dad once was, bravely acting like he thought a good soldier should in this situation. That was what he thought his parents would have wanted. So he ignored the screaming in his soul and said nothing to the nurse. Again, that's what a good soldier always does.

As I describe in detail in a later chapter, whenever Ricky told this story, he always told it with a heavy dose of pain and regret. In spite of his deformities, his parents always considered Ricky to be someone blessed with the gift of intelligence. I say blessed here, because there are far too many kids who are born to mothers that continued to smoke cigarettes while they were pregnant. Many of these kids also end up being born with more difficult mental or physical disabilities. Given all the many different disability possibilities, Ricky considered himself fortunate that he only had to live with two negative effects his mother's smoking had on his life.

While it is a choice for every mother, sometimes Ricky looked back on his own life and wondered how much better his life might have been had his dad interacted with him every night instead of his alcohol, TV, or sci-fi books, or his mother never smoked, so that he would be born with two testicles and no ADD. He also realized there are many other dads out there who never quit drinking, or mothers out there making that same choice not to quit smoking once they become pregnant. Many never realize, or in some instances, don't even care about, the effects that choice has on their child. Ricky just wanted to have the opportunity to live a life without fear, without ridicule, without being ashamed of who he was. Back when I knew him, I often reminded him there are some things in his life that a person simply can't control.

BASIC TRAINING

Two more major challenges in Ricky's life, not related to his mother's smoking, came in the beginning of 1978. They both had a profound effect on his life. First, Grandpa John, his only mentor to this point, passed away at the end of January. This loss hit Ricky a lot harder than his surgery. Grandpa John represented the only person in his life who cared enough to listen to him, to take the time to be by his side through the difficult challenges life already threw his way. His loss suddenly made life so much harder for Ricky. Being only six, he didn't know how to deal with the loss. Grieving the loss of a close family member wasn't something Ricky was ever taught about by his parents. His dad never talked about losing his mother, and his mom never said anything when Grandpa John passed away either. His grandpa from his dad's side, Vernet, lived three hours away so he was never around to talk. Ricky's limited intellectual understanding — typical for most six-year-old kids — was no help, and he had nothing else to rely on. So he did exactly what Ricky's dad did after his mom's passing: hide the pain inside, not speaking to anyone about it.

From then on, the only family member Ricky felt like he could turn to for emotional comfort as a child growing up was the family dog. Good thing for Ricky it was a Collie and not an attack dog. If the dog could talk, it might have been a good mentor for Ricky. Aside from his conversations with the dog, Ricky never talked about his struggles with anyone. Because he was taught to believe he only had intellectual gifts, Ricky had no basis for communication with either parent. For that reason, he quickly learned to emotionally suppress the pain he felt, which was a skill he mastered as he grew older. A good soldier always does.

Speaking of dogs, that was the second big challenge Ricky had to face, just over two months after Grandpa John passed away. He remembered the day well – March 31. What made it memorable was that day was a celebration of the fifth birthday party of a close neighbor who lived across the street. All the neighborhood kids were invited. Ricky's only chore for the day was to take out the garbage before going to the birthday party.

"Ricky, did you take the garbage out yet?" asked his mom.

"No, mom, not yet," Ricky answered.

"What are you waiting for, an invitation? You're not going to the birthday party until you've taken out the garbage."

"OK, mom," Ricky said. He then went to the kitchen to take the garbage out of the trash can under the sink.

Having secured the garbage bag, he lugged it downstairs and out the front door on his way to the trash cans. As he approached the trash cans, he spotted a dog about fifteen feet off to the side edge of the backyard fence. He wasn't a friendly collie like the family dog was, but most six-year-old children don't understand there are different types of dogs who respond differently when interacting with unfamiliar people.

"Hey there, doggy!" said Ricky as he hefted the trash bag into the can, cheerful at the discovery of another four-legged friend to play with.

The garbage properly disposed of, he walked behind the trash can, approaching his new friend. When he got close enough, he knelt on one knee, and extended his hand in a show of friendship to the nice doggy he wanted to befriend.

"Hey there, nice doggy! My name is Ricky. Would you like ...."

Before Ricky could finish his introduction, and with no time to react, the dog, a German Shepherd, angrily pounced right at his face, tearing off a huge chunk of flesh from the right side. Fortunately for Ricky, the dog missed biting into his right eye and the right side of his mouth by less than one centimeter.

After miraculously managing to run away from the dog without another attack, Ricky quickly slammed the front door behind him before screaming at the top of his lungs, "MOOOOOOOOOMMMMM!!!", while the blood continued to flow down his face and body. Once inside he couldn't go past the tile floor in the foyer, for even while bleeding profusely he wasn't allowed to stain the carpets on either the stairs leading upstairs, or the downstairs dungeon to his left where his monster/father often drank. Ricky imagined that punishment being more painful than the dog bite itself. There weren't any rags in the foyer either, only the unsanitary hairy pillow that served as the dog's bed. So all he could do was yell from the foyer as the blood continued to flow on to the hard tile floor.

"MOOOOOOOOOMMMMM!!! HEEEEELLLLPPPPP!!!", Ricky screamed again, the right side of his face now a bloody, mangled, unrecognizable mess.

"What's the mat ... OHHHH MY GOD!", shrieked his mom, seeing the mangled mess that was now Ricky's face for the first time.

Her first command was to his brother, as she ran down the stairs: "Go get me some paper towels for your brother! NOW! Honey, call 911! We have to get Ricky to the hospital!", barked his mom, giving everyone their assignments to help.

Ricky missed the birthday party later that day. Instead he got to enjoy his own party, sedated in a hospital bed. At least he got to enjoy ice cream, though he had to suck it (and everything else) through a straw until his face was restored to what it looked like before the dog bite, when he could eat normally again. In the meantime, he had to be brave. A good soldier always does.

Problem was, as told by Ricky, during the surgery no one came to join him for his party. Between losing Grandpa John two months earlier, and his parents' unwillingness to take the family to see him in his condition, the crippling loneliness of being in the hospital room made for several brutally agonizing days. It was much worse than the physical pain. Ricky recounts that while he didn't see his parents very often, they did stop by for a few short visits this time. Perhaps they realized they had to, now that they were the only responsible adults in his life after Grandpa John had passed away. The only consolation he got from the incident was an out of court settlement with the dog's owners for $4,000. Ricky received $3,000 of that and the lawyer representing him got $1,000 for his efforts. His parents put that money into a college trust fund for Ricky, which by the time he got to college twelve years later, was worth close to $17,000.

As for the surgery itself, his entire body had to be secured in an Indian stretcher. There are many different variations of Indian stretchers. This particular Indian stretcher was a long, polished wooden board with holes on the sides with which to slip thick leather straps through, which the hospital used to keep patients from moving – at all. Ricky's head and chin were each strapped tightly to the board by leather straps going through the board, the chin strap being carefully placed below the damaged area. The rest of his body was completely strapped in as well, especially his hands and arms, as he wasn't allowed to move them at all. For years, Ricky still cringed anytime he saw another stretcher, especially an Indian stretcher.

The medical team simply couldn't risk Ricky touching the surgically repaired face before it fully healed. So as not to undo any of the surgical procedures being performed, Ricky was forced to be completely immobile for the entire duration of the surgery. This is an extremely difficult task for a child with ADD, mind you – not that he had much of a choice while his face and body were strapped tightly into an Indian stretcher, twenty-four hours a day for close to a whole week. While that was difficult, the pain of being there all alone, with no one to talk to, made it so much harder.

In addition to all these challenges, Ricky also had to overcome having more pressure put on him as the first-born child. Ricky was told many times by his parents what being the first-born child meant. He was responsible for being the one to blaze a trail for his siblings through all the things he was required to understand and experience in life, so that he could pass on his experiences and wisdom, to make life easier for his siblings. Though Ricky was given the responsibility of being the family trailblazer for his siblings, Ricky was often envious of them. Thanks to his role as trailblazer, Ricky was never allowed to develop a personality of his own, like his younger brother and sister could. Being the trailblazer left little room for a personality other than the one decided for him as "the intellectual prodigy". The one thing he didn't get in fulfilling his role as trailblazer was support from his parents. His siblings got all of that instead. Because of the many ways he was given different labels than his parents: child genius, wimp, trailblazer, weakling, the only thing he got from his parents was neglect. All the support he was expected to find had to come from within himself, now that Grandpa John was gone.

According to Wikipedia, they describe neglect this way:

> "Neglect is a form of abuse where the perpetrator, who is responsible for caring for someone who is unable to care for themselves, fails to do so. It can be

a result of carelessness, indifference, or unwillingness and abuse.

Neglect may include the failure to provide sufficient supervision ... or the failure to fulfill other needs. ... Neglect can carry on in a child's life falling into many long-term side effects such as: physical injuries, developmental trauma disorder, **low self-esteem, attention disorders**, violent behavior, and can even cause death.

There are many different types of neglect but they all have consequences, whether it be physically or mentally. Neglect can affect the body physically by affecting a child's development and health, sometimes leading to chronic medical problems. Children experiencing neglect often suffer from malnutrition, which causes abnormal patterns for development. Not being given the proper nutrients at certain growth periods can result in stunted growth, and inadequate bone and muscle growth. *Brain functioning and information processing may also be affected by neglect. This may lead to difficulty in understanding directions, poor understanding of social relationships, or the inability to complete academic tasks without assistance.* ... Not only is neglect associated with physical problems, it also has an effect on a person mentally, ranging from poor peer relationships to violent behavior. Not only is behavior affected, but the way a person looks at themselves, *which can lead to low self-esteem and the feeling of being unwanted.* Neglect is more severe in younger children when it comes to psychological consequences. *Parental detachment can harm the child's development of bonding and attachment to the parents, causing the child's expectations to be the same when they get older* (furthering the cycle of abuse). *Too little parental availability can result in difficulties in problem solving, coping with stressful situations and social relationships. Studies of neglected children show heightened levels of depression, hopelessness, and higher incidents of suicide attempts."* [3]

Fortunately for Ricky, he never experienced the physical aspects of neglect. The neglect he experienced was mental and emotional, particularly the parts about parental detachment. Being alone for his two surgeries serve as a good example of the non-physical parental detachment form of neglect.

Now before you villainize Ricky's parents, I do know they did a great job in the physical aspects of raising him. He had good meals to eat, slept in a comfortable bed, lived in a physically safe home and neighborhood, was taught basic public etiquette and how to act responsibly at home, and was properly disciplined for doing things his parents considered wrong. These actions led Ricky and his siblings to develop values like respect for authority, honesty and the ability to behave with civility around others – most of the time. Unfortunately, that was the extent of the guidance Ricky received. In every other area, they took a hands-off approach, expecting Ricky to live up to his expectations as family trailblazer by figuring out everything else on his own. A good soldier always does.

Now while that sums up Ricky's relationships with his parents, next I want to describe how this upbringing affected him within the walls of the house he grew up in.

---

3   https://en.wikipedia.org/wiki/Neglect

3

Rules of Engagement

"Here is no one that will save you
Going down in flames
No surrender certain death
You look it in the eye
On the shores of tyranny
you crashed the human wave
paying for my freedom
with your lonely, unmarked graves"

"These Colours Don't Run", Iron Maiden

Being an intellectual in a physical family doesn't allow for many self-defense tools in the event of conflict. As much as he tried to display them, Ricky had no physical gifts. Those all belonged to his younger troublemaker / alpha male brother, who I'll call Robby. This led to a strong physical bond between Robby and their dad. As for emotional gifts, Ricky never got to develop those either. Redneck military family rules meant males weren't allowed to express emotional feelings, or develop strong emotional gifts, only females were. Ricky's mom and his sister, who I'll call Zariah, developed that close emotional bond that only females could. As for Ricky, guiding and mentoring him to develop and mature his emotional gifts was ... the family dog. As I mentioned earlier, both parents had a blue-collar mentality full of street and combat intelligence, but no book intelligence. Yet they still expected Ricky to function as the trailblazer for his younger siblings, armed with only the book intelligence he developed on his own.

Considering he was still a child, and his only books were his school textbooks, he didn't have a wide assortment of sources to develop his book intelligence. This becomes a major challenge when you lack the physical and emotional gifts needed to survive in a physical and emotional world. When you are also forced to live in a primarily physical and emotional family, having only intellectual gifts is as much of a burden as it is a blessing.

Even though he was the oldest, inside the walls of the house, Ricky was never given the freedom to act in a manner which allowed him to establish his own path in life. Making things easier for his siblings, while excelling in his studies to fulfill his parents' dreams of graduating college, were the only expectations he was required to live up to, with no exceptions permitted. So I don't get how Ricky's parents expected Ricky to be the trailblazer, while standing by and letting his younger brother become the alpha male of the family. I also don't understand how they could expect him to do so without any guidance at all. This left Ricky with no tools, save his largely undeveloped intelligence, with which to fulfill this high responsibility as family trailblazer.

As for his siblings, Robby was one year younger than Ricky, while Zariah was four years younger. As I mentioned earlier, Robby inherited all the physical gifts. In Herbert Spencer's world of survival of the fittest – which is what most schools are like in today's world, only the physically strong thrive. It is possible to interact with others using civility, but when survival of the fittest is the rule of law when it comes to interpersonal relationships, physical weakness and fear-based civility are as helpful as a spoon is for eating a steak. Since Ricky's home life was also governed by survival of the fittest rules, Robby's plan was to usurp the role of alpha male from Ricky by taking advantage of the physical bond he shared with his dad, and Robby was successful. Because Ricky's parents thought he possessed intellectual gifts, he was never given a chance to develop any physical gifts. He wanted to, to have some basis for a bond with his dad, but given his scrawny build, he was rarely given any reason to believe he should. His missing testicle and all the accompanying effects from that, the lack of focus from having ADD, along with all the effects of being neglected because of the chasm that was the difference between the white-collar lifestyle thrust upon him, and his family's blue-collar lifestyle, Ricky had so much working against him from birth. I should also mention, with regards to the neglect description from the previous chapter, Ricky also struggled to eat as much as his siblings. To compensate, Ricky's intake of liquids was much higher for a kid his age, so much so that his parents were concerned that this might stunt his growth. While I appreciated their concern, I had hoped they would have realized the underlying social neglect that was the root cause of his malnutrition. Sadly, they didn't.

Meanwhile, as Robby grew to appreciate his role of alpha male, the more he was encouraged by their dad to exert his authority over his siblings. Ricky was instead led to believe that being the alpha male had little value to an intellectual, so living in submission to the desires of his younger, stronger brother was a role he learned to accept. Why that was always baffled Ricky. I was often frustrated by the many ways in which it affected Ricky, most of which were negative influences.

Robby was also the troublemaker of the family. When you're the alpha male, you have to learn how and when to challenge authority. You also have to learn which rules should be enforced and which ones to challenge. As an example, according to what Ricky's parents told him, when they were both toddlers Robby discovered how to climb out of the playpen. He taught Ricky how to climb out. Ricky promptly displayed his new talent by climbing out, only to turn around and climb right back in. Unlike Robby, Ricky enjoyed life in the playpen because there were intellectually stimulating toys to play with.

For the most part, their dad thought Robby's antics were amusing. Like the time when Robby asked to borrow the nutcracker during a holiday meal one year. As he sat there waiting for it, dad quickly grabbed the back of Robby's head, then slammed it right into the nut sitting there in front of him on the table. Robby cried as everyone else looked on in shock. It was enough to crack the nut. Dad just laughed, which somehow further developed their bond as Robby grew up.

Now as alpha male, Robby was occasionally willing to fight back. Like the day Robby decided to get even with dad, hitting him in the rear end with the wooden spoon. Robby hit him so hard he broke the spoon. While Ricky was terrified at what their dad might do, Robby didn't care. Incidents like these greatly strengthened Robby's self-confidence. Because of Robby's physical gifts and the self-confidence that comes with them, his propensity to challenge their parents' authority and stand up to them occasionally came out of Robby. While it had a few disadvantages, the overall bond it created between Robby and their dad far outweighed the disadvantages. Even Ricky knew their dad had much more respect for Robby as a result of their mutual physical bond. That's how the alpha male mentality works. Many times Ricky wished his pathetic, scrawny figure would have allowed him some ability to physically relate to his dad too. He knew excelling physically was his only opportunity to develop a quality relationship with his dad. In reality though, as I mentioned many times, Ricky was simply too scrawny, and too terrified of his dad, to develop any bond with him. Though he tried far too hard for a child with his scrawny build, Ricky simply did not have many physical gifts. Those gifts only belonged to Robby. In spite of his efforts, not having those gifts affected Ricky's confidence growing up, though it didn't affect his continued efforts to try and develop that relationship through athletics, as I will discuss in later chapters.

As for Zariah, she was the female child Ricky's mom always wanted. Being the only female child granted her princess status. Being female also meant being granted the sole heir to the emotional bond with their mom. It was identical to the physical bond that Robby shared with Ricky's dad. As a male, even for someone as intellectually gifted as Ricky was, that gift of female bonding was not a gift Ricky understood. Same goes for Zariah's arrogance. Because she was raised with a princess mentality, she often used that status to her advantage. If she asked for something, she usually got it. Occasionally Robby tried using his alpha male status to control Zariah. He only ever got away with his attempts if their mom didn't step in to defend Zariah. She was the family princess after all. A few times, Ricky did try to get his mom to step in and defend him against Robby, the way she did for Zariah. Ricky quickly learned dad always sided with Robby, and mom always sided with Zariah. Largely due to his role as trailblazer and because of his advanced intellect, he rarely got any support from either parent.

As for bonding with his mother, Ricky did NOT try to develop anything there. He was too afraid to attempt it. His military-based, redneck family beliefs on things like incest, males who wear earrings, crossing gender barriers and same-sex relationships were absolutely negative, very strongly worded, and clearly defined. They also used coarse demeaning language towards people of other races, whether it was Hispanics, Arabs, Chinese or any other type of foreigner. It must have been either a redneck or a military way of thinking. Even Ricky's grandmother from his mother's side, anytime she came over to play cards, would always sing this little racist ditty to announce the beginning or end of her turn to play: "I go, you go, I see a dago." Ricky always thought she was saying "day go" to indicate time passing. It wasn't until he became a young adult that he discovered that "dago" is the equivalent racist term for an Italian, much like the n word is used to refer to blacks. Either way, Ricky never understood why his family chose to treat other ethnic groups differently. To Ricky, in their own way, they were verbally abused and neglected just like he was, so he could understand their plight.

Strict enforcement of rules was also of paramount importance to the soldier / family life within Ricky's family. To function in a combat environment, discipline was critical for making sure the soldier did what they were supposed to do and be where they were supposed to be. In the military, you either made the decisions, or you obeyed them. Feelings were irrelevant. Defeating the enemy was all that mattered. Harsh penalties awaited anyone who tried to act independently. Any attempts to express divergent personal opinions were also eliminated for the good of the military family. This was something Ricky discovered during his middle school years within his family's military squadron. One day he learned about Benedict Arnold and how he betrayed his country in school. He tried to explain what he learned about Benedict Arnold, politely explaining how he understood Arnold's motivating reason for doing what he did, as a subtle way of attempting to show that he too was being similarly rejected, snubbed, and shot down for his attempts to contribute his own individual ideas as part of the family. In response, his dad's military thought process immediately shot down any attempt at conversation regarding Benedict Arnold. To his dad, Arnold was a traitor to his country and that was the end of the discussion. Ricky never shared anything he learned in school with his family ever again after that.

Though his parents never abused him, he did get punished anytime he did something wrong. I am not writing this to debate the philosophical merits of whether or not to physically punish a child. Though Ricky never liked it, he and I both knew it was very helpful for his growth. Through it, Ricky learned to respect authority and grow from his mistakes. His fear of authority was also a source of motivation for Ricky, given the environment in which he was raised. As I mentioned earlier, his parents' favorite method was the wooden spoon to the rear end. Soap in the mouth to combat swearing was also used occasionally, like it was in the movie "A Christmas Story" but Ricky always wondered why he was being punished for talking just like his dad often did when he was drinking, just like Ralphie's dad in the movie. As a result, it was soon abandoned in favor of spanking as well. The discipline wasn't meant to intimidate the children, but it did serve its purpose of teaching them to try not to make mistakes, and when they did, to be accountable for them. Ricky was already more than afraid of doing anything his parents considered wrong, and didn't need any extra motivation to behave.

Since the Army was where Ricky's dad learned how to interact with adults, it influenced how he raised his children, Ricky included. His parents both lectured Ricky on how crying was for "sissies", and that if any of them were going to cry, they would give them something to cry about. He certainly didn't want to find out what that something was, especially after hearing that story about what a drill sergeant can do when challenged. A good soldier never cries anyway, or so Ricky was often told.

While not at school or doing homework, each of the children was responsible for assisting with chores around the house. Ricky enjoyed doing the indoor chores like dusting and vacuuming, and because it involved water, he also slightly enjoyed the aforementioned dishwashing. It wasn't fun when the water was scalding hot, and/or he had to wash them multiple times, in accordance with dad's fatherly wisdom. As for the outdoor chores, not so much. Helping tend to the backyard garden – weeding in particular – was the least favorite activity for both Ricky and Robby, which they were expected to do by hand every Saturday morning. Occasionally Ricky and Robby would both pretend to be asleep when dad came by to check up on them. Immediately after dad went back outside to tend to the backyard garden, they'd both quickly get dressed and take off to hang out with their closest friends down the street, whom I discuss more in a later chapter. Unfortunately, the garden still got weeded on Saturdays. It had to, so long as the boys expected to have a place to sleep and dinner to eat that day. If it meant doing it by flashlight, when it was too dark to see the weeds, then both Ricky and Robby had to pull weeds in the dark. It was the only option which granted them the right to be allowed back in the house to eat dinner or sleep in their beds that night. Both parents were uncompromising with this high standard, even if it meant doing the same chore over and over again, until they learned how to do it right. A good soldier always does.

———◆———

Earlier, I mentioned how Ricky was expected to figure out everything on his own. That pertained to life in public. Around the house, life was completely different. For most of Ricky's life prior to college, reality inside the walls called home consisted of little more than existence as a shadow of his parents. His desires, his dreams, his lifestyle preferences, his passion for success, and even - to some extent - his personality, were the intellectual property of his parents. As an example, when it came to the house stereo system, from the day Ricky was born, it was permanently tuned to the country music station, and no one was allowed to change it. Ricky finally got his parents to give in for the first time, over the Christmas holiday when Ricky was eleven years old. That discovery of rock music was a liberating feeling for Ricky, and the first time he got to enjoy the freedom of having control over something — anything — inside the walls of the house. More than any physical gift, that first taste of freedom from being forced to enjoy what his parents enjoyed, was the greatest Christmas present Ricky ever got from his parents. It all started with a little trip down "Electric Avenue" (by Eddy Grant), which is still one of Ricky's favorite songs, for obvious reasons.

At age six he was indoctrinated into an important family tradition: watching NFL football every Sunday. As a result, the following two unbreakable family rules regarding sports were very thoroughly established and ingrained in Ricky's head. Rule #1: Cheer for the New York Giants football team. As I mentioned previously, they are his dad's gladiatorial gridiron heroes. Rule #2: Cheer against the Dallas Cowboys, and become a one week fan of whoever they happen to be playing that week. They are public enemy #1 of Ricky's dad's heroes, and are never to be cheered for in any way, shape or form, with the only temporary exception being to need a Dallas victory to help the Giants make the playoffs. Those two rules were strictly enforced, as Ricky found out on Thanksgiving Day back in 1992.

This was Ricky's first year playing fantasy football while at college — there was money at stake for the league winner, $100 according to Ricky. Because of where Ricky got to draft, the top player left in the first round of his draft was Emmitt Smith, the Dallas Cowboys star running back. Ricky had to take him in order to have a chance to win the $100. So in spite of his family rules of football, he did.

Fast forward to that annual Thanksgiving holiday tradition spent at his uncle's house (mom's brother). The Giants happened to be playing the Cowboys in Dallas that Thanksgiving Day. In his desire to win the $100 prize that went to the fantasy football champion, Ricky openly cheered for Emmitt Smith against the Giants when he scored his first touchdown. Big mistake! The body language and cold stares of everyone else there spoke "mob mentality" to Ricky in a way he'd never before experienced. He tried to explain how the circumstances involved money / fantasy football, but they all quickly decided that was not a valid reason for breaking both of the two family rules regarding sports. So Ricky shut up. And cheered to himself. Unfortunately, Dallas won 30-3 that day. Emmitt Smith rushed for over 100 yards and had two touchdowns in beating their beloved NY Giants. Which was bad, of course, but it was good for Ricky's fantasy football team, though he couldn't say anything. Unlike Benedict Arnold, who was only given a disorderly conduct and fined a miniscule amount of fifty shillings, Ricky's betrayal of the family rules was considered high treason, and not to be repeated. EVER. Fortunately, nothing was said the rest of the day, but Ricky could still feel their collective hatred during the meal thanks to the Cowboys victory that day – it emanated from everyone at the dinner table like a legion of demons seeking to possess his very soul! Though it was a Thanksgiving dinner, no one seemed thankful on that cold, dreary, Connecticut evening after that painful football game they all just endured. For many years, that rivalry was also part of a war Ricky knew nothing about. As with everything else, he obeyed without ever questioning why. A good soldier always does.

In his efforts to earn some measure of respect from his parents, from as early as he can remember, Ricky tried his hardest to emulate their efforts by succeeding in athletics. His earliest efforts involved playing peewee soccer, but his parents removed him from playing because his efforts to exert himself on the field led him to experience heat exhaustion, which could have developed into heat stroke. He also played youth basketball, but wasn't any good at that either. Robby on the other hand, had the physical build and stamina to handle the rigors of playing football. Ricky was too afraid to play football, because he realized he didn't have the physical build or stamina to play. He was also too scared to be tackled hard by an opponent. The only sport Ricky was successful at was baseball. He and Robby both played on the neighborhood Little League team. I'll discuss the team's exploits in more detail in a later chapter.

His parents also made some slightly eccentric, dysfunctional choices with the children. So as to help them be well rounded, they also thought it would be best to have them learn to play music instruments. Perhaps they watched one too many episodes of the Partridge family. Ricky got the short end of the stick here too. In spite of his scrawny size, he was expected to be the drummer in the "family band". To this day, I still can't figure out why they were so insistent on this. Drums would have been the most physically demanding of the three instruments to play. Ricky certainly wasn't built for the rigors of that, given his scrawny build, propensity for heat stroke, and lack of endurance. They made him take lessons every week anyway. Robby was given guitar lessons so he could play lead guitar. Zariah was given both piano and singing lessons. It was also a contradiction emotionally, since it left Ricky (as the trailblazer) in the least recognizable position, while the guitarist and singer got all the notoriety for their talents. Since it was his parents' vision, Ricky never tried very hard to succeed at drums. His first instructor had as much personality as actor Ben Stein. His second instructor, Wayne, was much better, and lived down the street. Unlike his first instructor, Wayne had a personality that Ricky could relate to, which provided him enough motivation to continue learning to play.

Ricky's parents also had a strange sense of humor when going on vacations. Though he went to Disney World twice, Ricky most remembers going to a local fair in nearby Pennsylvania when he was around nine or ten years old. It started over 150 years ago as a celebration of the military. While this fair may have had good memories for many, Ricky and his siblings witnessed a mock hanging of some lady from the local history of this small Pennsylvania town. The parents thought it would be fun not to tell them it wasn't real until after they were traumatized. This resulted in frequent haunting flashbacks hijacking Ricky's dream life for years, further damaging his already weak self-esteem and self-confidence. In order to avoid the trauma involved with the pain of reliving an event like that, even if it was fake, Ricky had to bury that memory deep in his subconscious mind. A good soldier always does.

———◆———

During Ricky and Robby's transition from middle school to high school, personal computers were also becoming a popular item. Ricky and Robby decided to combine their allowance money for doing chores to buy themselves a Commodore-64 computer system. Initially, their parents insisted they purchase one educational game for every entertaining game, but as they figured out how to copy other games onto 5" floppy disks, the number of entertaining games far outweighed the number of educational games. They were also limited to how often they could play games, being permitted to do so only after their homework was done. This became another fun opportunity to interact with some of the other kids, but they both still preferred the outdoor activities. Ricky recounted how the educational games weren't very helpful. He most remembers a game that was supposed to teach him how to type with all five fingers, but unfortunately, Ricky never had the focus or hand / eye coordination to get very good at typing with all of his fingers. He tried, but eventually reverted back to the one finger hunt and peck method, which he used well into the late stages of his life as a young adult, before the consequences of his abusive past caught up with him.

"Listen earnestly to anything your children want to tell you, no matter what. If you don't listen eagerly to the little stuff when they are little, they won't tell you the big stuff when they are big, because to them all of it has always been big stuff." - Catherine M. Wallace [4]

I recently read an article about the merits of using "timeouts"

---

4   https://www.goodreads.com/author/quotes/219057.catherine_m_wallace

as a method of disciplining your children. The debate in the article dealt with whether it is acceptable for children under the age of five to be denied the opportunity to express their feelings, which being put in timeout usually does. In most cases it also eliminates the parent's willingness to explain to their kids what they did wrong and why it was wrong. Ricky never experienced a timeout, but with his parents' hands-off approach to raising him, most of his home life was one unending timeout. Ricky was rarely given any opportunities to express what he was going through, to learn and develop the social skills needed to mature into adulthood. As a result, once Grandpa John passed away, Ricky was only ever able to have meaningful conversations with either the family dog or I.

As a result, I often remember the many times Ricky shared how he wished his parents would have given him something – anything – in the way of guidance. The very core of his soul yearned for their help in leading him to understand himself through them. Sadly, though there were a few quality moments when he did receive the encouragement he longed for, they were few and far in between. Being able to learn and grow from the stories of his parents' past was something Ricky was never given the opportunity or privilege of having. His Benedict Arnold discussion was the most memorable incident. Most of the time, all he had to work with was what he saw and heard, which was second-hand information he had to process using his limited understanding. It certainly wasn't enough to be of any help, nor did it provide any lasting wisdom. Thanks to their hands-off approach to raising Ricky, what little guidance he did receive was based solely on discipline. When I compare Ricky to his parents, I'm still confused as to how or why, given that they both overcame so much in order to conquer their own worlds of "survival of the fittest" as children, why they never bothered to teach Ricky how to do the same.

As I mentioned earlier, like Lewis and Clark from American history, since Ricky was the oldest, Ricky was assigned the responsibility of exploring and blazing a trail that would make life easier for both of his younger siblings. Problem was, Ricky wasn't given any guidance on how to blaze a trail, or what trail he was supposed to blaze. He was never encouraged to ask for guidance, not that he believed either parent had the intellect (or the desire) to guide him anyway. The older Ricky got, the more he despised having to blaze a trail for his siblings with no encouragement or guidance at any point on the journey. After all, his parents thought that since Ricky was the first to experience life, he would be able to make life easier for them once they arrived where Ricky had already gone. In spite of having no idea where he was going, and nothing in the way of guidance whether or not he was successfully blazing this trail to this unknown destination, as always, Ricky tried his best. A good soldier always does.

Then again, when a person is repeatedly told his only gift is intelligence and he seeks encouragement from parents who don't place much value on intelligence, it's hard to open up to people on their terms. Equally difficult is the desire to share who you are, when you don't really know who you are, and the people whose authority you operate under, don't have the understanding or the desire to listen. Ricky's failed attempt to talk about Benedict Arnold with his family was a prime example. According to Ricky, around eighty-five percent of the time he lived as if his intellectual gifts meant nothing to his family. The other fifteen percent was when he was pushed to succeed. During those times, he was not given any guidance on what success was, how to succeed, or what exactly he was supposed to succeed in. All he was expected was to be the first family member to graduate college, then get a good paying white-collar job making lots of money. Like most everything else, he was left to figure the details out entirely on his own. A good soldier always does.

With Ricky, it was a good thing for his parents to discover his gift of intelligence at age three. Had it not been for his learning to read at an early age, he probably would have been told he wasn't good at anything. As I already mentioned, Ricky's parents were blue-collar rednecks. Neither had much in the way of intellectual gifts to offer Ricky the development and encouragement he needed. What his parents never learned – or applied – in how they raised Ricky was the understanding that gifts are not something a person develops on their own. Gifts, like people, are something that require mentoring and encouragement in order to properly grow. The only guidance Ricky ever had was the demeaning way they advised him that success meant working with his brain, not his hands the way his dad did.

Now I should mention that this isn't about blaming Ricky's parents for his upbringing. It is about using his story to show other parents the importance of properly developing and encouraging their children to discover their gifts, and to do so in a way that also develops their personal self-worth. Simply telling them they're gifted is not enough. Simply expecting them to graduate college and then get a good job with no guidance doesn't help either. In order to develop those gifts in someone else, it is extremely important to work to develop those gifts in yourself as parents, for the sake of your child. If you don't, should your child live long enough to make it to adulthood, rather than make their way into either a prison or a cemetery, they often end up being the types of adults that psychologists would label as "late-bloomers", with the cold, unforgiving streets as their guide in life. Those in this position end up being so far behind everyone else they don't fully mature until they're thirty years old, if not older. Most of them also end up resenting their parents, and possibly society, once they do start to bloom because their capacity to mature emotionally, physically and spiritually was suppressed and stunted for far too long. Which makes the process to maturity as an adult so much harder. Ricky had that working against him from the day he learned to read at age three.

My goal in sharing Ricky's story is to help parents understand that developing a stable understanding of the physical and emotional aspects of a person are just as important as their intellectual development. As I mentioned in the previous chapter, his parents weren't big on showing affection to Ricky. Adding to his confusion was his expectation of figuring out how to feel emotions such as compassion and kindness towards others entirely on his own, in environments where he was regularly, consistently abused for his deficiencies. The reality in Ricky's story is that neglect covers more than just the physical. The mental and emotional aspects of neglect are much harder to detect. In public settings, neglect never shows up, as most kids only put on a fake happy face. In light of what seems like daily incidents of violence in public schools or shopping malls, almost all of the kids / young adults who perpetrate these crimes have experienced some form of abuse or neglect in their life.

When these crimes do happen, physical abuse is not the driving force behind it. It's the emotional and mental abuse that goes along with it. For those that want to delve into the darkness of discovering why these kids end up taking the lives of their fellow classmates, the emotional and intellectual aspects of abuse and/or neglect are often the primary reason behind the instability. There have been many such examples of children's mental stability gone wrong, such as Sean Harris and Dylan Klebold from Columbine, CO; Jeff Wiese from Red Lake, Minnesota; Steven Kazmierczak from Northern Illinois; Seung-Hui Cho from Virginia Tech; Charles Andrew Williams from Santee, California; and Adam Lanza from Sandy Hook, NY. Those are just the more prominent ones. There have been hundreds of others not mentioned. As I described in Chapter 1, Ricky also went much further down that road of darkness than most people even think of traveling. As a result, I get to be the one to tell you his story instead. The fact that Ricky's name is not among the long list of murderers mentioned above, doesn't make his story any less important. I do hope it will wake people up to the reality of how abuse and/or neglect, in one form or another, is the root cause leading these youth to inflict the same emotional pain they feel on as many other people as they can.

As a result, whatever civility Ricky did possess, was based solely on fear of being disobedient of his parents' expectations. When that fear dissipates, and courage eventually develops in its place after being set free, that is when the doors swing open and society finds out what type of person that child becomes. In Ricky's case, the effects of neglect in the non-physical aspects of his upbringing led Ricky to discover the hard way just how damaging neglect can be, when the doors to his soul swung open for everyone in his life to see, as I described in the opening chapter.

Some of the stories I share on Ricky's behalf were hard for Ricky to talk about during his life. I mention them to show what type of person that neglect might produce: a borderline psychotic maniac with little to no understanding of how to function holistically as an adult in the real world. A world in which I am discovering that far too many kids are completely unprepared to enter as adults. Unfortunately, this deficiency in his home life affected Ricky's ability to cope with the largest and longest challenge he would have in his life: navigating life within a public school system. I will especially focus on how his role as "family trailblazer" played out in the type of education he received. As the trailblazer, again his only stated mission was to make life easier for his siblings so that when they attended school after him, school would be much easier. Being the intelligent one in the family, his parents thought he could easily handle this role without any guidance. What they didn't realize was how this mission left him no room to develop a personality of his own. I've already described what family life was like for Ricky, and how not getting any guidance severely stunted his ability to express himself with any semblance of maturity around his family, and how being the omega male due to his physical size left him with no understanding how to stand up for himself. This made school a much bigger challenge, which will become brutally clear in the next chapter.

4

Subdivisions

> *"Subdivisions ... in the high school halls,*
> *in the shopping malls ... conform or be cast out ...*
> *Subdivisions ... in the basement bars,*
> *in the backs of cars ... be cool or be cast out"*
>
> *"Subdivisions", Rush*

I recently heard about an online video dealing with a high school boy who was bullied by a fellow classmate. The story was told by the boy's mom, who spoke about the abuse her son endured before committing suicide. She spoke about how her son was bullied by a fellow classmate because of his scrawny appearance. When the son asks his bully what he did to warrant being bullied, the bully responded, "because you're a pussy who needs to get his ass kicked". A short time later, prior to committing suicide the son posted on Facebook that he was considering suicide. The bully replied with the challenge to, "man up or shut up". This certainly isn't a unique experience, as a simple online search for suicides resulting from being bullied will show hundreds of similar examples. I used to think children knew better, but with more and more kids being abused the way Ricky was, I'd like for nothing more than to see all youth have a brighter future where they make a positive change in the lives of their fellow classmates, rather than hear them talk about encouraging suicide as an act of manliness. Without this positive change, many of these kids end up bringing weapons to school to hurt and/or kill fellow students, like some of the names I mentioned in Chapter 3.

My heart broke at the thought of someone being so cold and ruthless as to encourage someone to commit suicide as an act of manliness. For those of you that have compassion, I'm sure you feel much the same way. For Ricky, life in high school was much the same for him as it was for the son that committed suicide. As they both found out the hard way, when the doors to culture swing open to allow in relative morality and/or survival of the fittest as common-sense beliefs, bullying others follows that belief to its logical conclusion. My point is not to debate the weaknesses of relative morality vs. religion in public schools, but rather to open the eyes of parents / adults to the problems it causes with impressionable teenagers. The endless news reports of violent teenagers shooting others, illustrates how many bullied teenagers quit caring about life in this world.

Like the son in this story, in addition to the loneliness Ricky felt at home, school was also a daily exercise to overcome life in an abusive environment where he was perceived as weak by all his fellow classmates. Ricky received much of the same level of compassion and concern for his well-being as this unnamed suicidal student did. In elementary school, Ricky was regularly referred to as monkey ears and/or dumbo because of the size of his ears. He was clearly smarter than the rest of the students based on his ability to grasp what was being taught, and as is typical of a survival of the fittest culture, putting others down for their differences is always easier than looking to help in their growth. Those that perceive themselves as inferior only need to throw out a few well-placed insults to bring the smarter kids down to their level. It's a lot easier than looking to the intelligent ones to help them develop, as that requires a lot more effort. This attitude was especially on display during recess, where Ricky's wimpy nerd status always meant being the last one chosen when it came time to pick players for team activities like kickball, in spite of his status as the fastest kid in his class. I remember all the stories Ricky told about how demeaning it felt being the one kickball player no one wanted on their team, and how often he cried at being the last player chosen each time a team sport was played. Ricky also learned that most public school teachers do little to keep the abuse from occurring.

For the next few years of elementary school, there were twin siblings who used survival of the fittest rules to run recess. The male's name was Ray and the female's name was RaeAnn. Ray was mellow, rarely fighting unless necessary, but RaeAnn was the volatile one who made a sport of chasing down anyone she felt like beating up, and gender didn't matter. She could beat up most boys or girls. If she couldn't beat up someone by herself, she got Ray to help her, but that was extremely rare. She was built like a bowling ball, and could run as fast as one. Her only redeeming quality is she didn't care who she abused. She often tried to catch Ricky, but rarely did, thanks to the fact that he was one of a very small group of kids who could outrun RaeAnn.

Even the teachers overlooked Ricky's gifts. In sixth grade, around ninety percent of the students were chosen to be safety patrol officers on the buses. For Ricky, being chosen finally meant being respected amongst his classmates for a change. When that selection day came, Ricky was crushed to discover he wasn't chosen. The only day he did get to work as a patrol officer was on his twelfth birthday, while all the chosen patrol officers were rewarded with a special field trip.

In middle school, he got sent home from school his first day because his parents chose to have him wear a lime green tank top shirt with matching green shorts. He found out that hard way that this was not the middle school dress code. As the year wore on, his missing testicle meant being pointed and laughed at every time he had to adjust himself while performing some form of cardiovascular exercise in gym class, such as basketball or soccer. It was here that Ricky first discovered the embarrassing implications of having said no to that plastic testicle after his surgery. Every time he exercised, he was forced to deal with the stigma of being ridiculed for having only one testicle, because of all the constant discomfort associated with the deformity. The only thing more difficult was avoiding having to explain why he kept having to adjust his gym shorts, for fear of even further embarrassment. On top of that, he still had his ADD and his scrawny build working against him. It also meant being relegated to a forced association with the social misfits, thus ending any possible chance of having anything resembling a dating relationship. Not that his social status would have mattered, since he was equally clueless when it came to understanding dating, having never been taught anything about male / female relationships by his parents. This includes never having been lectured about the birds and the bees.

In most schools, the most likely path to popularity and success is through excelling at athletics, as a player for the boys, or cheerleader for the girls. In every school, they are the ones that schools always use to showcase the best and the brightest of students. Even Ricky grasped school politics enough to know this was how the school hierarchy was set up, hence the desire to please his parents via a pursuit of an athletic career. In addition to his scrawny build, he also had the added stigma of being more prone to heat stroke and heat exhaustion. As a result, his parents decided not to have him participate in too many high aerobic sports like soccer and football. He did get to play little league baseball with most of the neighborhood kids. In seventh grade he made the soccer team by default because the soccer team comprised all the kids who weren't man enough to play football. Because he wasn't able to handle the rigors of running, a mutual agreement was reached so that he could play defense. Playing defense meant only playing one specific area and being primarily responsible for keeping the ball from getting past you in that limited area. It also meant limited running up and down the field, preventing Ricky's heat stroke from getting the best of him. Ricky's responsibility was the left third of the field. For those not familiar with soccer, the field is divided into left, middle and right. Ricky was the starting left halfback. In spite of being a team of non-football castoffs, that seventh grade team excelled. Highlighting the team was the state's leading goal scorer, and an all-state goalie. Before there was such a thing as concussions, the goalie would get himself fired up by slamming his head against the side of the bus while listening to heavy metal rock music. The surprising part is that the bus frame almost always lost the battle. While Ricky's talent wasn't anywhere near that, he did manage to have his moment of glory in one game that year, helping the team preserve a win – sort of. In the first half of the game, a player from the other team was driving down Ricky's side of the field, kicking the ball hard in an attempt at a long pass to one of his teammates. Ricky successfully managed to prevent the pass from reaching the teammate, but only because the ball drilled him right in the head, knocking him unconscious. Once play was stopped, his teammates had to drag him off the field, and revive him with smelling salts, or whatever it was they used to help him so that he could be effective enough to get back on the field and help the team win. Again, there were no concussion protocols for head injuries back then. In the second half, Ricky did manage to return to play at his assigned position as left halfback. As the game clock was about to expire, with Ricky's team holding on to a one goal lead, an opponent was driving the ball down Ricky's side of the field. Realizing he had to attempt one last hard shot from about thirty yards away from the goal before time ran out, this player did just that. So in a moment of heroic glory, Ricky prevented this opponent from getting this last second shot past him. Ok, so maybe it wasn't quite heroic glory, but he did manage to block the shot – by getting drilled in the head a second time, again knocking him unconscious. As a result, Ricky was carried off the field by his teammates as a hero, not because of his skill playing soccer, but because in his state of unconsciousness, he had to be literally carried off the field. I know Ricky would have preferred to remain conscious to celebrate with his teammates, while also remembering what happened. Not quite the way to earn one's only moment of athletic glory, but when you're as lacking in athletic skill as Ricky was, I suppose you enjoy it nonetheless.

In the state championship that year, which Ricky prayed not to have to play (and his prayers were answered), the opposing team allowed ninth graders on their team, while Ricky's middle school only had seventh and eighth graders. Some of the ninth graders on the opposing team were five to six inches taller and about twenty to thirty pounds bigger than Ricky and his teammates. While the game was close, Ricky watched from the bench as his teammates had to make regular trips to the sideline due to injuries, largely from the aggressive play by their opponents, taking advantage of the age/size difference. In spite of the punishment Ricky's team endured that day, the game was still tied 1-1, until the other team scored the winning goal with fifteen seconds left to win the state championship 2-1.

Later that year, Ricky tried out for the baseball team. Based on his experience playing Little League, which I discuss in more detail in the next chapter, he knew he was good, so this was his big chance to showcase his skills at first base. He probably should have also tried center field because of his speed, but he figured first base was where he could shine. He really gave it his all, believing he was the most talented first basemen out there. Unfortunately, he didn't make the baseball team. He was crushed again. It was a rejection from which it would take him years to recover. He wanted to tell someone about it, but he already knew from past experience he had no one to share his heartbreak with at home or at school. Crying was still a sign of unmanliness that only sissies did, so the soldier in him held in the pain of not making the team, which was all he could do.

In eighth grade, he started out the year playing soccer again, but it didn't feel the same this time around. Still reeling from not making the baseball team, his interest in excelling in school also began to wane. Gone was his best shot at being a star athlete, making his parents proud of him. After the heartbreak of not making the baseball team the previous spring, his interest in athletics rapidly dissipated as quickly as his interest in school itself. As a result, his grades began to drop. In response, his parents prevented him from playing sports until his grades improved. That only further ruined his desire to succeed, since he didn't play sports again until he played baseball the final semester of his senior year of high school.

Helping his decision there, was his most memorable experience in middle school – the class field trip. Each student was placed four to a room at the hotel they were staying at. The trip was a two-day trip to Washington, D.C. to experience the sights within the nation's capital – Lincoln Memorial, Washington Monument, the Capitol building, and the Smithsonian Museum, among others. While the sights were memorable, they paled in comparison to the constant three on one abuse Ricky endured in the hotel room, from the time they walked in the room until they all went to sleep. For Ricky, crying until he ran out of tears as he was relegated to sleep on the floor, was the only thing that helped him sleep during the trip. He wanted to say or do something to defend himself, which would only have made the abuse worse. He didn't have any allies here to turn to.

In high school, because of his intellectual gifts, in spite of his poor grades in eighth grade, his parents placed Ricky in the high honors classes. This did grant him some measure of respect, as his classmates were all part of the "in-crowd" – the best of the best students in school. In spite of being in the in-crowd, he still had the outcast personality, and the notoriety that goes with that unfortunate reputation. So in that spirit, his "friends" did get a bit more creative with showing him how much they valued having him around. Ricky especially hated lunch in the cafeteria, as his in-crowd "friends" often made him feel just as welcome as everyone outside of his circle of "friends". Especially annoying was when the song "And She Was" by Talking Heads was played on the cafeteria jukebox, which was quite often. The song had a brief drum beat at the end of each line of the chorus, and all the others at the table would all play it with their hands, with the concluding beat being for all of the others to simultaneously smack Ricky in the head – some harder than others. The humiliation of witnessing everyone else in the cafeteria seeing this happen on a regular basis was the only thing more painful than the head slaps themselves.

For those outside his circle of "friends", his reputation as omega male from middle school followed him to high school, even though he now hung out with the in-crowd in school. He didn't want to spend too much time with the other social outcasts, for fear of being looked down on more, though they were the people he most understood and who understood him. He chose to be the punching bag for the in-crowd students instead. At least with them, he had some measure of social respect, or so Ricky believed.

In reality, since his "friends" rarely offered him anything in the way of social acceptance outside of lunch, the rest of the school had the same freedom his "friends" had, namely the freedom to abuse him as often as they desired. Whether it was in the hallway or before the start of some classes didn't matter. Ricky always had that target on his chest, visible to everyone but him. Ricky's least favorite method of torment, and the one he most often dealt with in high school, was returning to his locker only to discover that it was broken into. It had a lock on it, but most of the students knew how to break into any locker, even with a lock on it. So Ricky would often return to his locker and unlock it, only to discover all his possessions had been removed, with only a note left in its place. The note would instruct him to go to another empty locker, where he would find another note directing him to a third empty locker, and on it went with anywhere between at least eight more notes, if not more. So as to be able to swap out books for the next class, this game was one he had to play, which also meant dealing with more criticism from the teachers, after finally showing up five to ten minutes late for quite a few of his classes. He occasionally thought about the possibility of carrying all his books with him. Not being physically strong enough prevented that idea from becoming a reality, so a wall locker was a necessity. No matter where he moved his locker, eventually his anonymous abusers found whatever new location he used to keep his stuff, even in the most remote parts of the school where no one ever went. His "friends" never stood up for him. Since it was a public school, none of the teachers who had the privilege of witnessing the abuse never did anything either. Ricky literally had no allies in school, not even his own brother. All the while Ricky was still expected to be the one to experience everything first for the sake of his younger siblings, while still being held to the highest educational standards by his parents. That was what the soldier in him was expected to do, or so he imagined. He certainly never got any guidance to convince him otherwise.

Until he was able to drive himself to and from school, he wasn't able to develop any strong bonds with the other students because of the distance from school. The school was a good eight miles west of his hometown, which meant having to forego most after school activities in order to catch the bus home, unlike the kids who lived close to the school. There was a second bus that drove kids home an hour later. Given all the abuse he endured during normal school hours, another hour of that was never something he was going to stick around for. The only exception was the rare occasion where he was punished with detention for having done something wrong. The bus ride was equally demeaning, since he was also everyone's favorite target for being bullied on the bus. After his first week of initiation, and given all he had to endure at school, the bus ride was a light version of the abuse he endured in school, since it only lasted for about twenty minutes.

His social standing with the women in his school was the only area where his status was worse. He had no prior dating experience, and nothing from his parents in the way of knowledge on the subject, unless you count the adult magazines (Playboy, Penthouse, etc.) he and some of his neighborhood friends found when they were teenagers. To ensure they wouldn't get taken away, they swapped covers with the one magazine that was designed for them as kids, making sure to tape the adult magazine to the inside cover of their kids magazine, so that the tape was not visible from the outside. So when the parents thought the boys were reading their children's magazines, they were instead checking out the adult magazines. In order to protect that secret, none of the kids ever revealed what they did. For those that have tried this approach, I apologize for spoiling the secret. Parents, please disregard this paragraph.

As a result of this deficiency, when Ricky got to high school and was expected to learn the art of dating, he mostly avoided the subject. Part of him was terrified at the thought of being humiliated by a girl once she discovered he only had one testicle, forever ruining what little social status he did have. The two times he did attempt to ask someone out, he ended up getting embarrassed by everyone at school, which only confirmed his fears, after which he avoided any further attempts to even think about asking anyone else.

Most others didn't even know who he was. For the homecoming football game his senior year he drove to the game to hang out with his "friends" to see the team play what would be the only football game Ricky ever watched, even considering his brother played on the team as a linebacker. The rest of the family never made it a point to attend the games as a family either. As Ricky sat there enjoying the game, a female named Erika sat down at the other end of the group and introduced everyone she knew. When it came time to introduce Ricky to her friend, she quietly muttered to her friend, "and I don't know who that is", as if Ricky wasn't able to hear her say that. That accurately summed up the notoriety Ricky had amongst his classmates.

His senior year, he did get asked to the prom by a female from his class named Vicki, but turned her down. He didn't think she was serious, nor did he think she really cared about him. After all he'd been through thus far, his mind pictured this as just another attempt to humiliate him, only this time in the most revered social gathering where everyone who was anyone was there, and where being humiliated would sting a lot worse. So he never attended prom.

The one thing Ricky never got from anyone was support. As I mentioned earlier, his parents decided to punish Ricky for his poor grades by not allowing Ricky to take part in any after school activities, particularly sports. This punishment was meant to convince Ricky to focus more on doing better in school. It accomplished the exact opposite, completely destroying what little desire Ricky still had left to please his parents, or anyone else for that matter. To Ricky, school now represented a vast social and educational wasteland with no positive reason for achieving anything. His parents abandoned him to figure everything out by himself, his classmates were mostly abusive jerks (his brother included), he had no athletic future with which to win his dad's approval, and he spent most of his time trying his hardest to avoid being ridiculed for all of his physical and social inadequacies. The people he called "friends" in high school did nothing to help Ricky either.

In eighth grade, all these social deficiencies led Ricky to manifest anti-authoritarian behavior for the first time. Ricky didn't remember what it was about, but one day one of his teachers was getting angry with all the students, so Ricky simply blurted out that she was being a bitch. Right there in front of the class. It was probably the only time he stood up for others. It did earn him a momentary badge of respect, as well as a trip to the principal's office. Sadly, aside from being a safety patrol for his twelfth birthday, and when he was knocked unconscious twice in that one soccer game, this was the only time he was ever treated with respect in school. The rest of the time, all the abuse developed in his soul an emotional fuse that led him to eventually become that ticking time bomb I described in Chapter 1 – one that would eventually blow up in grand fashion, if it wasn't diffused before it exploded. This is also a common theme for the many other children who end up committing either suicide or murder-suicide.

By the time he got to high school, the pieces of the time bomb in his soul continued to assemble. Ricky failed in his search to find a single reason to continue to strive to excel in school. He started the year in high honors biology, with a decrepit old hag for a teacher, in a classroom that always reeked of formaldehyde. She was in her mid-80's and was still teaching, mainly because of her reputation as a highly renowned science textbook author. While she still had the name recognition, her memory and her ability to teach was failing, probably because of the formaldehyde and all the mysterious caked on junk that lived at the bottom of her coffee mug. All the students saw it whenever she left it sitting out, which was often. Everyone figured it was some chemical formula that she needed to continue to permit her a few moments of alert clarity amidst her semi-catatonic state. No student ever dared to touch the mug, for fear of whatever chemical reaction would have afflicted anyone who did – something to the effect of having your finger instantly dissolved. Given the discoloration of the mug, and the formaldehyde smell of the room, all the students decided this was a realistic possibility.

Meanwhile, because of her failing memory, she always referred to Ricky as Albert. Albert happened to be another student from a year or two earlier that shared the same last name as Ricky. So Ricky struggled to succeed in her class and got a D the first semester. Since this was his first taste of high honors classes, his lack of focus due to ADD made keeping up a real challenge. At home Ricky had to deal with the almost constant nagging as to why he would disgrace the family by getting a D on his report card, which meant he was failing to live up to his parents' genius expectations by succeeding in high honors classes. In response, his parents decided to move him down a level to honors chemistry. After dealing with all the pressure at home for getting a D on his first high school report card, he quit trying. He no longer cared. Each week, the primary assignment for honors chemistry was to find an article having something to do with science – it could be anything at all – and write a one-page paper about it. Because he didn't care anymore, Ricky ignored this weekly assignment, so he was given an F in his second semester of high school. Initially, getting an F had no effect on his thoughts or emotions, though it led to a lot more pressure as to why he would dishonor the family name by failing. The only thing it really taught Ricky was that he had to do his best to go through the motions of trying to pass his classes, to keep his parents off his back. So for the last three and a half years of high school, school meant little more than doing just well enough to pass all his classes, to avoid the heavy stress of failing to live up to his parents' high standard as a "genius". By that point, all he wanted to do was fly under everyone's radar and graduate. Any additional honor he might have received for doing well no longer meant anything to him. Since no one was ever willing to offer any support to accompany the expectations of being someone with high potential for success due to his intelligence, coupled with all the abuse he had to endure without anyone ever standing up for him, he simply lost all desire to try living up to everyone else's expectations. Since Ricky still had his parents verbal abuse waiting for him at home, he had to put in some effort in school, so he did just well enough to graduate with passing grades. He had already experienced far too many instances of feeling worthless within his family for not living up to everyone else's expectations, expectations which always led to what Ricky knew were only compounded by regular abuse from his classmates. Beneath the surface, Ricky wanted no part in any of that anymore. He just didn't have the freedom to openly tell anyone or rebel.

Along the way, one particular incident Ricky recounted from his time in high school was the day he and his "friends" were having a discussion at the lunch table. It was a philosophical discussion about whether or not it is possible to prove anything exists. The antagonist in the conversation, a musically talented student named Andre, was casting doubt on any argument Ricky would make trying to prove certain things existed. Now Andre was also a hemophiliac, which means when he bleeds, the blood doesn't clot very quickly. After realizing the futility of being philosophically shot down by Andre at every turn, he gave up arguing, walked behind Andre and stabbed him in the back of the neck with a pencil, then walked away.

The way I see it, in all these incidents, Ricky's fellow students had to fill their need to validate their existence and make them feel important at his expense – typical behavior for a survival of the fittest world. Sadly, when life at a public school exemplifies the cultural concept of survival of the fittest, this type of behavior is a common occurrence. In order to survive, physical strength and/or athletic abilities are the most important ingredients for success. All other gifts are useless without physical strength, which explains why the jocks are always the most respected members of school society. In spite of everything working against Ricky – undiagnosed ADD, the fear of being discovered as only having one testicle, always being at the bottom of the social strata in school, not being permitted or physically big enough to play sports, having to walk this road entirely by himself without any support, and the high expectations placed on him since he first learned to read, he did somehow manage to graduate high school. That he got to that point at all without snapping and/or committing suicide was a miracle in itself. This led to some measure of gratitude from his parents, as that meant Ricky was able to take the next step in fulfilling their dream for him to be the first member of the family to graduate college. Notice I did say their dream. Graduating college and getting a successful white-collar job was his parents' dream for him. Ricky gave up on that dream after getting that F in honors chemistry, but never had the freedom to openly tell his parents. As a result, his high school diploma was nothing but an empty achievement to Ricky. Even after giving up inside, he was never taught to dream for himself – his future as a college graduate and successful business executive was already one his parents had decided for him, so that Ricky wouldn't have to dirty his hands in the blue-collar world like they did.

Until he graduated high school, however, Ricky still had to deal with the daily abuse associated with a learning institution that held the key to his future – a future he had no idea how to pursue, with absolutely no family support in helping him make it special. So for those teachers that happen to work for a school or other education institution, help out the Ricky's of your school. They may have a situation at home that is really challenging, or hate being bullied by classmates but have no idea who to trust, or they may not have any adult mentors to guide them to know what to do. It might prevent that student from committing suicide, or worse yet, bringing a gun to school and shooting fellow classmates as an act of revenge, both of which seem to be the two favorite options for kids like Ricky, who feel like they have no other choice.

Now if anyone out there has a son or daughter being abused, or is a teacher with a student who you know is being abused, take the time to teach that child to develop the skills needed to mature in this brutal world, and teach them to dream their own dreams – for themselves. Without someone who cares, they'll end up becoming another Ricky, which seems to be an increasing trend among students in today's survival of the fittest world.

5

'Hood Life

> *"Now Main Street's whitewashed windows and vacant stores*
> *Seems like there ain't nobody wants to come down here no more*
> *They're closing down the textile mill across the railroad tracks*
> *Foreman says these jobs are going boys*
> *and they ain't coming back to your hometown"*
>
> *"My Hometown"*, Bruce Springsteen

It was one of a diminishing number of backcountry outposts in northern New Jersey, likely the closest one to New York City. To locals like Ricky who grew up in this backcountry town, it was a flood prone, lifeless farming town surrounded by big cities, rivers and major freeways eager to take you anywhere, so long as the rivers didn't act up and prevent a chance to escape. According to FEMA, sixty-eight percent of the town is located in flood prone areas, mostly due to being bordered by a river that splits into two rivers, which form the boundaries to the south and east. [5]

---

5   https://www.lincolnpark.org/194/FLOOD-INFORMATION

It ranks second in the state of New Jersey as most flood-prone city. Building new properties can't help the town, as the only places left to build are in the sixty-eight percent of town that's flood prone. As a result, the overall population is still just over ten thousand, even though it's been thirty years since Ricky left there to attend college.

There are only four ways out of town – US 202 would take you east or west out of town to the nearest major expressway – Interstate 287 to the west, or NJ Route 23 and US-46 to the east. Taking the back roads to the north also led to Route 23. If you were really brave, attempting to leave via the southeast corner of town to get to Interstate 80 or US-46 was a possibility, but considering the rivers' unpredictability, that was like driving into the mouth of a dragon. Very few townsfolk ever attempted it regularly. Going north or west were the only reliable ways out of town, regardless of what direction you needed to go. The only big chain stores brave enough to venture an effort at business success in the town's history have been McDonald's, CVS and Walgreens, and none even dared venture inside the city limits until the very end of the 1980's. Looking for the corner of happy and healthy? Not likely to find it in this town, unless a tranquil escape from the chaos of big city life was your definition of happy. In that case, it was everything you could ask for, so long as the rivers didn't act up.

The center of town was a real small triangle, probably less than one square mile, with traffic lights marking the three points of the triangle. In order to make it big in this world, you had to find a job or own a business – somewhere else. The ideal location for doing that was in the urban, civilized world only thirty miles away – the tri-state area in and around New York City

– if the rivers permitted safe passage eastward. For many, the train or the bus were much more reliable, and could get you to and from work without having to worry about the flooding or worse, the traffic. With a train you got home from New York City in time for dinner. If you were foolish enough to drive, the drive took around thirty minutes – without traffic. With traffic, three to four hours was typical. Not that making it back to the backcountry paradise that was Ricky's hometown offered much to come back to. For the city slickers working in New York City, the contrast in lifestyles (and the floods) served more as a warning not to come back, but still they kept coming back. US Highway 202 cut right through the middle of the town, which was also the only legitimate reason it was even on the map in the first place. Even the signs leading people in or out of town via 202 led people to get easily lost. If you ask Ricky, he'd tell you that getting lost and avoiding his hometown was probably a good thing.

The town only ever produced one star – former Miami Dolphins running back Jim Kiick. His mother Alice lived up the street in the 'hood as well. She was Ricky's first grade teacher, and she too was a strict disciplinarian, where many a misbehaving hand got smacked by a ruler. It may well have been the same house Jim was born and raised in, but Ricky never found out. Alice was very private and didn't leave the house much, and Ricky was taught not to intrude. When Ricky was born, Jim was flourishing in his role as running back with the Miami Dolphins.

Growing up in this backwoods outpost was another aspect through which life was totally enigmatic for Ricky and many other kids like him growing up there. Living in a backcountry town surrounded on all sides by bigger cities and flood-prone rivers left Ricky confused. He was expected to fulfill a successful future as a business executive, but was never given any understanding of life outside his dead-end town. As I mentioned earlier, Ricky never had any legitimate guidance on how to go about discovering there was such a thing as a future outside the city limit signs. At the same time, he was expected to make it big in a big city environment he rarely got to experience prior to leaving for college. Only in fantasy shows like the Beverly Hillbillies do backcountry folk somehow make a high-income living in the big city.

Running parallel to US-202 were railroad tracks. As with most other towns, most families were identified by which side of the tracks you lived on. If you lived on the south side of the tracks, you probably lived in a flood prone area. The north siders didn't really have to deal with it much, unless you lived on the northeast side of town. Very few north siders were poor. So the south side was 'hood life, and the north side was 'good life. As a result, the southsiders were more likely to be the troublemakers around town, for when the rivers overflowed, most of their lifestyle stability was swept away with the current and drowned.

Ricky grew up as a southsider but he lived in a 'hood just south of the tracks. It was right smack in the center of town, hidden amidst all the freeways that surrounded it on all sides. While it was technically part of the 'hood, given the proximity to the center of town and the infrequency with which the houses flooded, it more resembled the north side of town, which was a blessing for the families within the 'hood Ricky and his friends called home.

Ricky was equally blessed to have many neighbors, most with

boys who were within five years older or younger than him. If given the choice, Ricky would have preferred to spend all his time with them, in spite of how crazy they were. In the 'hood they all had the freedom to be themselves, with no fear of ridicule. The rest of the boys in the 'hood – around twelve of them – would often be available for whatever the activity of the day was. While I won't go into too much detail about each of them, out of respect for what they meant to Ricky, they all deserve some mention out of gratitude for the positive effect their friendships had on Ricky when he was here.

Their closest friends were the three Ice boys – Jimi, Jeff and Joey. With Ricky and Robby rounding out the group, the five of them were always the core group that decided what sport was played on any given day. Jimi – the oldest – was named after the late guitarist Jimi Hendrix, and in spite of being the leader by default, had a very mellow personality. Jeff, who was Ricky's age, was the crazy one, often instigating trouble in his family, in much the same way Robby did. As a result Robby and Jeff shared that same bond as alpha males. Joey, who was three years younger than Jeff and Ricky, was also the omega male of his family, which led to a close friendship between he and Ricky during their pre-teen years. The rest of the core group all had their own unique personality traits that helped them gel as part of the group.

Carlo was a tall Italian kid a year older than Ricky, and the tallest regular member of the group, in spite of his average build. Like Jimi, he had a very laid-back personality, the only difference being he would always be up for whatever the game of the day was. Carlo's mom Rose, and Ricky's mom were close, in spite of the fact Rose was a heavy cigarette smoker. Carlo's clothes always reeked of cigarette smoke, as did his entire house. Being in their house for five minutes was probably the equivalent of smoking a pack of cigarettes yourself.

The Sly boys – Todd, Craig and Matthew, were strict Dutch Reformed Christians who, for religious reasons, weren't allowed to come out and play on Sundays. Craig was clearly the most athletically gifted kid in the neighborhood, and also the same age as Ricky and Jeff. Matthew was too young, and his mom didn't want him getting hurt, so he was rarely allowed to join the rough games, and Todd was never the athletic type, except for when it came to basketball, as his height of around 6'4" meant he was the tallest member of the 'hood. Anytime he played basketball he had a major advantage, which led the rest of the group to not invite him to play basketball because of how lopsided basketball games were when he did play. He wasn't into any of the non-contact sports like Craig was.

Gregg was a chubby kid a few years younger than Ricky, who was always available to be part of the games. He wasn't very athletic, but he always had a good attitude about everything and always fit in with the personality of the group. Of all the people Ricky respected the most during his teenage years, Gregg and Carlo were at the top of the list.

There were the Twiggy brothers – Mark and Matt. Mark was Jimi's age and rarely joined the group due to age difference, but Matt lived up to his last name. Paper thin and barely over 4' tall, Matt was probably the only kid scrawnier than Ricky. His main attribute was his speed, an ability that always made him a worthy opponent to challenge Ricky in sprinting contests. The most memorable contest Ricky recounted was the time where the group decided to set up a series of races to determine the fastest kid in the 'hood, and one particular race in this series had a special surprise located immediately past the finish line – a thick patch of rose bushes. The goal of this particular race was to decide who had the courage to forego personal safety in order to win, or risk losing by protecting your body from the thick line of rose bushes past the finish line. Sprinting through the finish line, on the other hand, meant running into the rose bushes at full speed, requiring much assistance in eventually being freed from all the thorns – slowly of course – by everyone else. For most races, Ricky could pull away far enough to allow him to slow down enough to avoid the rose bushes and still win. But the championship race against Matt was a different story. So when he faced Matt in that last race to determine the neighborhood champion, he wasn't willing to surrender his title to anyone. Matt chose to slow down and lost, but Ricky chose to run full speed into the rose bushes just past the finish line. His title of fastest kid in the 'hood wasn't one he was willing to let anyone else claim. It was a sharp decision Ricky got to make on his own, one of the few he got to be proud of around the 'hood. Thankfully all those pointers he received helped him maintain his status as fastest kid in the 'hood.

John was a Chinese kid whose left hand only had a thumb and one big, deformed finger. In spite of only being around 4'6" tall, he was built like a freight train. Having John participate meant having a miniature rugby player involved. When tackle football was the game of choice, the most feared person wasn't Jimi because he was the biggest, nor was it Robby or Jeff because they played pee-wee football. The most feared football player was John because he could take the hardest hit from anyone, where the person trying to hit him frequently got hurt a lot worse than John. Food wise, John never turned down an opportunity to enjoy a hamburger, mainly because all his parents ever cooked was Chinese food, which he was sick of, but could never tell his parents that. His parents didn't speak very good English either, unlike John.

Brian had skin color matching his last name, and he and Robby were close because they both played pee-wee football. He got along with Ricky and Robby because of his knack for games, especially role-playing and card games. One particular game Brian developed with Ricky and Robby was the unguarded waist game. If you left your waist exposed and vulnerable, the other people present would try to backhand you in the stomach as hard as they could. The most memorable incident was a time the house phone rang at Ricky and Robby's house. As Ricky sat down on his parents' bed to reach for the phone, Brian took advantage of the distraction, successfully backhanding Ricky as hard as he could in the stomach. His timing was superb, leading Ricky to yell into the phone receiver he picked up a moment earlier, "OWWW, F*&%ER!!!" instead of your standard, "Hello?". Figuring it was safer that Ricky not continue to find out who was on the other end of the phone line, he paused to stare at the receiver momentarily before quickly hanging up the phone. He also hoped whoever it was wouldn't call back, because answering the phone a second time moments later would have been really awkward. Thankfully, there was no second call, but I can only imagine the conversation this person would later have with one or both parents, regarding this strange phone introduction / quick hangup. Once he got off the phone, he turned his full attention to Brian for revenge. As the only colored family in this racially diverse neighborhood, their skin color didn't hinder their ability to fit in to 'hood life, but there were two exceptions.

The first was Chris. Living across the street from Ricky and Robby, Chris was an Italian Catholic who ended up attending a well-known private Catholic high school. It was Chris' fifth birthday that Ricky missed because of the dog bite. Prior to high school he was a big part of the group. Once he got to high school, his new classmates at his Catholic prep high school taught him to hate blacks like Brian. Because of his newly discovered racist beliefs, he mostly became an outcast to the group, since he would often demean Brian and anyone else who had darker skin. Everyone else still valued each other around the 'hood, but thanks to Chris' new attitude, he no longer valued people like Brian because of his skin color. Most of the kids still hung out with him occasionally, but were wary of his newfound racist attitudes, so they all used caution anytime they hung out with Chris.

The second exception were the Dice brothers — Joe and Pete. Also Italian like Chris, they were never part of the boys in the 'hood. Their attitude was much more racist than Chris', and the word around the 'hood was their family dealt drugs. They always seemed to be hanging out with other families who had that shady Italian mafia look to them. Because they were also racist, the younger brother, Pete, once tried to beat up Brian, only to himself get beat up instead. Robby later beat him up too because he heard Robby was willing to stand up for Brian. Everything about their attitude matched the hood's perception of them, which is why none of the other parents allowed their kids to play with them. Joe was around Ricky's age. While he wasn't big physically, Joe allied himself with the trouble kids around the hood, and there were a small group of them that lived up the hill. They usually hung out in "the woods", a small wooded area to the left of Ricky's house. Wanting to maintain their tough troublemaker image, anyone outside their group who dared go in, usually got hurt. Only Robby was ever brave enough to go in there. He came out with ketchup on his clothes, but did his best to convince everyone else it was blood, only without the bruises you get from getting beat up and cut. Most of the kids knew it was ketchup, but it didn't change the fact that no one else was ever brave enough to go in and find out for themselves. While Ricky was away at college, Joe later got arrested for beating up a police officer, which didn't surprise anyone – except maybe the police officer. If you watch TV, Joe has been in the news recently for being an illegal citizen about to be deported back to Italy. He and his (ex-?) wife happen to be stars on one of those real housewives shows on TV. To the rest of the boys in the 'hood, none of them would have been surprised to see how Joe turned out as an adult. He was just as much trouble during his youth living in the 'hood.

The 'hood later had two additions to the group, named Bobby and Mikey, who moved in when most of the kids were around twelve years old. Mikey was only around eight at the time – too young to play, and Bobby's only real gift was getting on everyone's nerves with his stupid insults. Most of the other kids didn't much care for Bobby, but if an extra player was needed, he was always available.

Occasionally there were others who joined the group. Mike, a black curly haired kid Ricky's age who didn't usually try to be part of the group. He often thought of himself as being too good and too talented for the 'hood life. Paul, who lived next door to Chris, was Carlo and Jimi's age, but was never really part of the group, though he did join the group occasionally. There was also a kid named Chance whose parents were divorced. He occasionally visited his dad – who lived next door to Paul – sometimes on weekends, but he lived with his mom during the week.

Last was Ricky's next door neighbor, Little David. He was built like John, only taller, but was mentally impaired the same way Ricky was physically impaired. Little David's impairment often manifested in a distorted, humorous view of seeing other people experience pain, whether from his hands or someone else's. When it was from his hands, his lack of awareness he was doing so made everyone else cautious around him. As an example, he once went on a campout with the boys from the 'hood, and after seeing others rough house, decided to put another kid in a bear hug, squeezing this poor kid so hard, his face turned purple. Because of this, having him join the group was often too risky, given his unstable mental state and his lack of understanding of what it meant to be a part of the group dynamic they had as friends.

There were a few girls around the neighborhood too, but they were never part of the boys in the 'hood. The boys never wanted to include girls in their activities for fear of injury, and because they never needed to include them due to the number of boys they already had.

Like most close-knit neighborhoods, it also had its challenges, in the form of the unemployed town drunk – I'll call him JS. He lived between Little David and the Sly family, two houses to the right of Ricky. He had no job, and never maintained his property – house or yard, and had a German Shepherd for a pet. Most of the folks in the neighborhood believed the dog crapped in the house and the unkempt backyard on regular occasions. For all these reasons, all of the kids were forbidden to step foot on his property. The only time he was ever seen was when he sat outside late at night drinking heavily (and his outbursts were worse than those of Ricky's dad) or playing his guitar, but no one ever paid him any attention.

Aside from that, thanks to the number of kids his age and the bond they all developed, Ricky did live in a somewhat stable social environment where most of the kids in the 'hood knew each other. ... somewhat being the key word. They all had the same level of maturity as Ricky. Living in a backwoods town known mostly for rivers with the vast majority of land owned by one farming family, the backwoods environment of the town and the flooding didn't make for kids who sought after maturity or wisdom. Testing the body's limits for pain, on the other hand, was commonplace among them. Scrapes and bruises from bicycles or sporting contests were badges of honor around the 'hood, as were trips exploring any undeveloped parts of town with off-road bicycles. Ricky had plenty of stories to share. I won't share all of them, but these are some of the more shocking ones.

"You gotta let me come in so I can hide ... Jimi is chasing me around the neighborhood with an axe!" passionately exclaimed Jeff, terror coursing through every word out of his mouth. Ricky's mom was the first one to hear the loud banging on the door that fall Saturday morning. While Jimi had the axe, odds are it was Jeff that did something to Jimi to warrant that response. As an alpha male like Robby, Jeff was also an instigator of trouble. Because Ricky and Robby knew the Ice brothers so well, the concept of one of them chasing another one around the 'hood with a weapon was entirely realistic. As evidence, Ricky once mentioned how he was playing Dungeons and Dragons with Joey and Jimi at their house. Jeff wanted to join in but was turned down by Joey. Five minutes later Jeff comes back with a steak knife, pointing it near Joey's throat while demanding to play. Ricky sat there stunned, as would most kids. Jeff did join in that day, but Ricky couldn't help but wonder ... if he did something Jeff didn't like, would he get the same treatment? At the time of Jeff's frantic pounding on their front door, Ricky happened to be downstairs watching TV in the living room – the same room where the drunken monster lurked most evenings. Upon hearing the banging on the door and the conversation between Jeff and Ricky's mom, his eyes stared deeply into the painted hand stuck in the window. It was the symbol representing the neighborhood watch program, and as he longingly stared at it, he pondered how thankful Jeff must have been at that moment for a neighborhood watch program. The Ice boys were typical of most other 'hood families, all of which seemed to have some trait that set them apart from what was then considered normal family life. In their case, they were raised by a single mother, divorced from a father who was a police officer. Ricky never knew if the father was abusive before the divorce, but given their dysfunctional actions, such as chasing siblings around the neighborhood with axes, one might possibly draw that conclusion. While Jeff's tactics often worked with his brothers, he knew better than to try anything like that around the rest of the group. As for what happened between Jeff and Jimi after Jeff eventually decided he no longer needed to hide, Ricky never found out.

18 AND LIFE

Now there were many times where the collective group decided that normal sports occasionally got boring. So they experimented with new ways to play them – the boys in the 'hood were always open to trying new sports. The most extreme version was soccer baseball, or playing baseball using a soccer ball instead of a baseball. It was there the boys discovered how much harder it is to hit a soccer ball far. They also discovered how much of a kickback a baseball bat has when you hit a soccer ball with it. It was one of the few occasions Robby ran home screaming bloody murder, in much the same way Ricky did when he got bit by the dog. The participants all learned a valuable physics lesson: when an object in motion contacts a stationary object, that stationary object assumes the velocity of the moving object. In English, when a thrown soccer ball hits a stationary aluminum baseball bat, the bat continues in motion until it contacts the forehead of the person holding the object ... HARD! Robby had to get quite a few stitches that day once he did finally sprint the five-hundred or so feet down the street to get home and get his gash taken care of at the hospital. Not to be outdone, Ricky also recounted the time when Joey did something to anger Jeff in Ricky's house. In his efforts to help Joey get away from Jeff's close pursuit, Ricky made his way past the door leading into the garage, quickly closing it behind him on his way into the garage. Because of the close proximity, Jeff slammed into the door at full speed, breaking his nose in the process.

The Ice boys also had a pool in their backyard, overlooking their back porch. The boys would often come up with unusual tricks to make jumping into the pool more exciting. Their cat Rusty was often included in the challenges too. It was here that Ricky was able to witness the opportunity to see Joey get

Rusty to do a two and a half gainer into the pool before letting out a large hiss to accompany the release of his claws, moments before he contacted the water. Naturally, Rusty didn't much care for the pool, much like Ricky didn't care for school. But they frequently tortured him with aquatic challenges anyway. That's the type of kids they all were when together.

At the time Ricky was growing up, there was a big farm running alongside US-202 to the east of the 'hood, with farmland on both the north and the south side of US-202. In the winter, on the south side of the farm to the east of Ricky's house, was a big hill that dominated the rest of the southern landscape of town. It was often the place where anyone around town could go sledding. Since it was close to the 'hood, and Ricky's family had the best sleds, they got to decide who joined them every winter. Now the hill had two levels. The lower level, a stretch of about three-hundred to four-hundred feet, with a one-hundred to one-hundred and fifty foot elevation, was fully cleared of trees and made for some good sledding in its own right. Beyond that point the hill continued another fifty to one-hundred feet uphill, but required more skill to sled past, as there were many trees one would have to navigate to make it to the open sledding area. Of course the core group was brave enough to navigate the trees, as it too was a sign of bravery and skill to avoid the trees, or a badge of honor to sled into a tree. It was a win-win for their crazed passion for a greater challenge, and a greater thrill. No one ever shared the injuries they suffered at the hands of the trees – no one wanted to lose out on a chance to continue their high-risk efforts to sled through the trees successfully. This worked well until that fateful day when Matt Twiggy again lived up to his name and slammed into a tree, cracking a few ribs in the process. Everyone's first thought was to figure out a way to hide Twiggy's injury from the parents. Their goal was to not mention it so they could continue to be able to sled through the trees. The boys soon realized this injury was too severe to hide from the parents, so when word got out about Twiggy's rib injury, as expected the parental council in the 'hood all decided to ban anyone else from any further sledding forays through the trees.

Aside from sledding through trees, all of the parents let their kids do what they wanted during play time. Running full speed into rose bushes, tackle football, street hockey, basketball, soccer baseball, or neighborhood bike races were all acceptable activities to keep the kids occupied. Thanks to the rivers and how it affected the financial lifestyle of its' residents, the crime rate in town was low so being kidnapped or robbed was highly unlikely – there simply wasn't any reason to do either as the town wasn't known for prosperity. Even at night, the fear of being out late at night didn't exist in the 'hood. Minor injuries were common. If anyone got hurt, so long as it didn't involve something serious like a severe gash from a baseball bat to the forehead, a broken nose from running into a door at full speed, or cracked ribs sledding into a tree at a high rate of speed, they were bandaged up but still free to go out and play on. Given the bond they all had, and how injuries were badges of honor, they often did continue playing.

Any other outdoor activity was allowed, and when the call came (either a loud yell or a phone call to a neighbor's parents) to head in for the night, the call was always heeded within thirty minutes. If ignored, that meant losing the freedom to go back out for a week or more. The rest of the time was solely for the boys to do whatever they wanted around the 'hood. This bond was one that did wonders for developing good people skills. It was also the type of environment where they learned to treat each other like people, one where social status wasn't divided into categories and people weren't expected to be defined by their physical strengths or weaknesses, like in school. Everyone fit in and no one ever looked down on anyone else.

These days, most kids don't live in 'hoods like the one Ricky did. The culture of fear has certainly permeated even most rural neighborhoods, mostly due to fear of crime. Kids don't go out and play anymore. Backyards are almost always fenced in, and woodlands are off limits. Aside from those who play sports, most children don't get to adventure in the real world anymore due to the increase in crime in schools and neighborhoods. Besides, the virtual world of video games is a much safer world in which to play in today's culture. While it is safer, it prevents children from understanding how to develop interpersonal relationship skills. Even Ricky would have testified to this, as the 'hood was always a safe place to try stupid things and develop close bonds with others who were in the same situation as he was. It may not seem important, but letting your kids get out and experience life for themselves outside of the house with other kids like them is an extremely valuable part of an effective adult life. Looking back, were Ricky still here, I know he would have wanted to see more kids develop those interpersonal relationships within their neighborhood, because as Ricky discovered the hard way, school is not always the best place for kids to develop close bonds with others. The increase in suicides and school shootings only verifies this claim. Encourage your kids to spend time outside with other neighborhood kids their age, to discover what life is like outside the home. It may seem dangerous, given the increase in crime in the world, but so is kids bringing guns to school and shooting up classmates because they fail to develop any meaningful, positive relationships. Those that don't have those relationships, or even for some that do – like Ricky – feel trapped and learn to distrust those around them, which they continue to do as adults. For those in urban low-income areas, the environment may be different, but the opportunity to have positive meaningful relationships is equally possible. It all depends on the involvement of the parents, by giving the kids the opportunity to discern the difference between good and bad friendships, and help them understand the importance of each, without weapons. When you lose those attributes, it removes a child's ability to experience the positive values of close friendships, as well as the opportunity to allow the kids to experience the freedom to explore what life has to offer – wherever they live.

Around Ricky's hometown, those that lived in the more flood prone parts of town had a tough persona. They had to, as living in flood-prone area made for some strong wills. Ricky once hung out with a kid from that part of town he knew from school. Like Ricky, he was also twelve at the time, but was twice as big as Ricky. So when this friend threatened to beat Ricky up if he didn't smoke a cigarette with him, Ricky fearfully caved in. At the dinner table later that night, Ricky was so racked with fear, sweat drops were forming around his face until he finally confessed he had smoked a cigarette earlier that day. With the typical military discipline that he knew to expect from his parents for such an egregious offense, Ricky was grounded for two months.

Through this experience, Ricky learned he needed to be careful who to trust. Not everyone who claimed to be his friend had his best interests in mind. He knew the rest of the boys in the 'hood wouldn't make threats like that, as they all knew and respected the bond they had with each other, largely because of the aforementioned desire to value each other solely as equals, regardless of size or intelligence difference. It also reminded Ricky that as with school, outside of the 'hood he didn't really have any true friends.

Around the time Ricky turned thirteen, the town gradually began a transition to a big city environment, as did the neighborhood chemistry. The farm directly behind Ricky's house was sold. In its' place a condo complex was built, to accommodate the need for additional housing for people commuting to and from New York City. With the growth of technology and vehicle travel accommodating those young adults that worked in New York City in the middle of the 1980's, the expansion was necessary. JS's house was condemned and razed, as were the woods next to Ricky's house, with new houses being built in their place. The sledding hill also lost its' appeal, as the hill was a lot shorter, with the end of it now being a small paved road at the top of the apartment complex. Avoiding cars was now more of a challenge than avoiding trees. As the transition from rural to urban was taking place, the chemistry in the 'hood changed drastically, when the Ice boys moved to California. Wanting to give them a chance at a free college education at a state school for California residents, their mom decided that was in their best interests as the condos were being built.

After they moved, Ricky and Robby did keep in touch through letter writing with the Ice boys for a little while, but life just wasn't the same without them. The remaining kids still played games together during their high school years, but tackle football was hardly ever played after their departure. Ricky developed a closer friendship with Carlo and Gregg, Robby usually hung out with Brian and Craig. Chris was occasionally part of Ricky's group, but because of his racist attitude, he was excluded from any combined activities to prevent another fight between he and Brian. Occasionally they would get a few kids to play baseball, basketball or street hockey, but without the Ice boys, their numbers rarely hit double digits. The field that they played most of their sports on happened to be the middle school practice field, with an outdoor basketball court there too.

Even after the Ice boys left for sunny California, life in the 'hood helped Ricky develop some close friendships growing up, though life wasn't all negative outside of the 'hood. There were two positive influences, albeit minor ones, in his life. The first will be the subject of the next chapter.

6

Holy Roller

> *"Holy roller, lookin' down*
> *Where you think you know all the answers*
> *Arrogance and pride are sin*
> *Better look to your own chances*
> *Holy roller, can you save your own soul?*
> *Can you save your own soul?*
> *Holy roller"*
>
> *"Holy Roller"*, Nazareth

"The roof of the church will fall on your head if you enter a Protestant church!" This was the belief instilled in Ricky's mom when she was a child. Being from Sicily, Roman Catholicism was heavily practiced by Ricky's maternal grandparents. In spite of the superstitious warning, she ended up marrying a Protestant anyway. For the record, the roof did not fall on her head for having done so. Ricky occasionally wondered what alternative punishment might be in his mom's future for breaking this religious superstition by marrying a Protestant. Could there have been an exception made in her case? As a result of this "unholy matrimony", his mom did the unthinkable and took her rebellion one step further – she herself became a Protestant! Ricky always imagined what grandma might tell him regarding what the punishment was for that. Based on his fantasy adventures playing Dungeons and Dragons, Ricky imagined it being something to the effect of having the whole church implode around her, creating a huge sinkhole in the ground that would one day lead the whole family right into hell. Despite the superstitions instilled in Ricky's mom by her parents, the family settled on attending the local Reformed Church of America denomination, or RCA as it is known in evangelical circles.

Ricky also wondered if that punishment would affect him as the first-born child, if it hadn't already. He believed in the possibility that his physical deformities were divine punishment for her poor decision whom to marry, and later become, a Protestant. As with every other aspect of Ricky's life, he wasn't made to feel like he could be open and ask anyone about his religious questions. Doing so usually ended up with him being made to feel stupid for asking. As a result of these superstitious beliefs, Ricky also occasionally wondered to himself what might become of him when he grew up and had to himself decide whom to marry based on a similar list of authorized religions from which to find a wife. His parents had already decided what his career path would be. Church attendance every week was also a requirement, with the only exceptions being either hospitalization or debilitating illness. So for Ricky, it wasn't much of a stretch for him to imagine having to live up to similar strict restrictions regarding a girlfriend / wife, were he to eventually attempt to date. Any perceived superstitions about religion affected his ability to date someone outside his faith. He believed his parents would probably decide were he to eventually try to date – someday. He also imagined what potential punishment awaited him for failing to adhere to similar superstitions he didn't know about, to keep him in line spiritually. Fortunately, thanks to his secret regarding his missing testicle, his lack of understanding how to relate to women, and his status as social outcast, he had no courage to cross that bridge and attempt to date a female. The embarrassment he dealt with, the two times he tried to ask someone out in high school, pretty much ended his desire to even try anymore.

The concept of religious superstitions did influence Ricky's thought process with his first crush back in middle school, a cheerleader named Allyson. As a practicing Jew, she was the darling of Ricky's school. Everyone adored her, especially Ricky, and she had her pick of anyone she wanted to date. She was even voted middle school class president of Ricky's 8th grade class. He dreamed about asking her out, but for all the reasons I mentioned, he had nothing in the way of courage to actually follow through.

Now this wasn't the only way his parents' religious upbringing affected life for the children. Friday evening dinners were also heavily influenced by his mom's Catholicism – the term Catholics use for this is a "macro-snapper". What that means is that any kind of meat other than fish is not to be eaten on Fridays. In case you ever wondered why most restaurants feature fish on Friday evenings, now you know. Sometimes the meals were good, like when they had fried flounder with homemade macaroni and cheese. That was one meal Ricky certainly looked forward to every week. Other times, they had to endure disgusting concoctions like tuna noodle casserole with cold, diced celery. Ricky believed that adding cold celery to a main entrée was the easiest way to ruin the taste of a meal. While I've never actually tried it, I think it sounds gross as well! Celery only belongs in a salad, or with peanut butter spread over it. As for options, prior to receiving an allowance, their options were to eat what mom made or not eat until Saturday morning. Once they were given an allowance, on those repulsive nights when the home kitchen served tuna noodle casserole, they all went out for pizza instead — usually with a meat product other than fish! Thankfully there was no superstitious punishment for eating meat on Fridays using their own money, for his parents never explained what the punishment for violating this religious superstition was, and it was not enforced outside the home.

The Christmas Eve dinner meal had similar religious significance, and was one everyone looked forward to. It was called the Feast of the Seven Fishes, where the seven fishes were served with an endless supply of pasta with two types of sauces: marinara or an aioli sauce. As for the religious significance of the feast, writing for the New York Times, author Melissa Clark explains:

> "It's a Southern Italian (and now Italian-American) custom in which a grand meal of at least seven different kinds of seafood is served before midnight Mass. The fish part comes from the Catholic practice of abstaining from meat on Christmas Eve, while the number may refer to the seven sacraments. Or it could be the Seven Hills of Rome. No one is sure, but the tradition has stuck fast." [6]

---

6   Clark, Melissa. *Surf's Up on Christmas Eve*. New York Times. December 16, 2013. https://www.nytimes.com/2013/12/18/dining/surfs-up-on-christmas-eve.html

Wikipedia adds this about the religious significance of the meal:

> "The tradition comes from Southern Italy, where it is known as The Vigil (*La Vigilia*). This celebration commemorates the wait, the *Vigilia de Natale*, for the midnight birth of the baby Jesus. It was introduced in the United States by Southern Italian immigrants in New York City's Little Italy in the late 1800s. The long tradition of eating seafood on Christmas Eve dates from the Roman Catholic tradition of abstaining from eating meat on the eve of a feast day. As no meat or animal fat could be used on such days, observant Catholics would instead eat fish (typically fried in oil)." [7]

Now Clark explains that the meal usually consists of seven different courses, with each course featuring a different type of fish / seafood. In Ricky's house they saved time and effort by putting all seven meats into the pasta sauces. Those fishes were: clams, scallops, shrimp, oysters, squid, mussels, and anchovies. There was also an alternative made exclusively for Ricky's maternal grandmother. It was made without anchovies, since she didn't like them because she thought they were too salty. For her they also made smelt as a replacement.

As for the church they all went to, it was located just up the street from the town middle school, also within walking distance from the 'hood. It wasn't a large building, but on a typical Sunday it could host around 200 attendees. For the three special holidays where even the most worldly of believers showed up – Christmas, Mother's Day and Easter – more seats could be added to the adjacent auditorium to seat another 300 or

---

7   https://en.wikipedia.org/wiki/Feast_of_the_Seven_Fishes

so people. On those days attendance was still beyond capacity, with many finding themselves having to stand for the service.

The senior pastor there when Ricky was born was a humble Dutch pastor named Bill. Bill was hired as senior pastor back in 1952, and retired from his role as senior pastor in 1983. He was a strong family man, with a faithful wife named Pearl, and two children, who had long since started their own lives away from home, long before Ricky was old enough to know who they were. Ricky thought Bill's style of preaching was a bit on the dry, boring side, as would most pre-teens hearing an adult sermon, but any deficiency in his preaching style he made up for with his Christ-centered humility and his ability to relate to the people on their level. This was equally true with his relationship with the children who attended Sunday school. Since Ricky spent most of his time in Sunday school, he only had to endure Bill's boring sermons during the summer, when Sunday school was not in session. The Sunday school calendar observed an annual schedule similar to regular school – September to June. He still appreciated Bill for his humility, and was a good person to emulate, albeit indirectly.

When Ricky was an infant, like most other infants who were children of members or regular attendees, he was baptized. Since the sanctuary was small and the funds were limited in the backcountry church, all the baptisms performed there consisted of sprinkling, not immersion. From there, once Ricky reached kindergarten age, he was required to start Sunday school, which was the religious equivalent of kindergarten, only in church there was no demeaning abuse. The church also had different classes for different age levels, ranging from kindergarten all the way to high school seniors.

As for the requirement to attend Sunday school, the family vehicle left for church sharply at 8:45 am every week. If you didn't make out to the vehicle prior to its' departure time, for whatever reason, you had to walk the half-mile to church by yourself to avoid being punished for not attending. The most memorable example of being left behind, was the first time Robby missed the family ride and had to walk to church. He showed up in the middle of the popular hymn Onward Christian Soldiers being sang by everyone present. While searching for the rest of the family, Robby walked right down the center aisle crying so loud it drowned out most of the adults singing. I especially found that ironic personification of a brave "Christian Soldier" quite entertaining!

As a reward for regular attendance, similar to earning a Varsity letter on your jacket for playing sports, if you went the whole year of Sunday school with two or fewer absences, you earned an annual pin. The rewards stacked so if you made it through two straight years you got your first year base, and a second year wreath that attached to the outside. Years three+ meant getting annual bars that would be attached to the bottom of the wreath. As a result, neither Ricky or his siblings ever missed getting a pin. Since Sunday School only lasted from age five to eighteen, a fourteen year pin was the highest you could get, which all of them earned. It wasn't quite as prestigious as earning a varsity letter award for sports in high school, but it was a reward to honor the regular attendees. As an example, wearing them openly while attending public school provided an additional reason for someone to verbally, or possibly physically, abuse you. Given all the abuse he'd endured, Ricky knew to avoid any additional reason through which he might receive more abuse, so he never actually wore them except during

Sunday school graduation week. That week of Sunday school, usually in June every year, they each received another annual pin awarded in front of the main congregation.

The Sunday school activities were fun, for the most part. Each week offered a different game. The one Ricky remembered most was the Bible verse finding game, since he was almost always the first one to find Bible verses. They did offer other contests too, like making ten consecutive free throws out on the basketball court after the instruction part of Sunday school. If you could do that you got your name on a wall plaque in the church. The leadership called it being in the "Big Ten Club". Many other activities were offered every year to give the kids something to be proud of, as a way of providing a solid religious upbringing, in ways that kept the kids interested every week.

Helping his ability was a decision he made when he was nine years young. He figured he'd want to know about this book he was required to learn about every Sunday, so he decided to read the whole Bible from cover to cover. This turned out to be the only good decision he made on his own as a child, and the only one he felt motivated to do on his own. Surprisingly, his parents supported his decision. Since he was always labelled a child genius, this shouldn't have been much of a challenge for him. He did complete it before his tenth birthday, at which time he promised to read it cover to cover every ninth year of his life. I hoped he would have studied it more frequently – it might have helped him through all the challenges life threw his way.

Given that religious family environment, the last thing Ricky needed was more criticism at home for daring to trust someone outside the family for life guidance, whether it be pastor Bill, or anyone else. Attempting to find an adult mentor at church was verboten, since Ricky thought asking would have made them look bad as parents. He was especially worried how talking about his inner fears and challenges would lower his mom's paragon standing in the church. Any activity or discussion that involved his parents meant using extreme caution with whom he told what, because of the possibility that it would only lead to more punishment at home.

While the moral lessons were helpful, and the activities fun, because of all he went through outside of church, it didn't give him any tools to overcome the problems he faced in school and at home. He never learned the importance of prayer, or what it meant to trust in, or have a relationship with, Jesus as Lord. Because of his mom's high standing in the church, he didn't know if anyone there would serve as an adequate mentor for him. He wanted to ask, but given how his mom was close with most everyone in the church, in the end Ricky chose not to risk asking anyone. His dad wasn't much into church. He only went because he had to set an example as family patriarch every Sunday morning. All the times he used the name of Jesus or God as swear words around the house the rest of the week, provided clear evidence he was never much into religion.

When Pastor Bill retired in 1983, a new pastor was hired from Michigan. His name was Fred and he was a stocky man of German descent, who was a great storyteller. Fred was a husband to a wife named Paula, and had two daughters. Ricky most remembers being captivated by his story of a German cobbler named Papa Panoff. Fred's sermons were much more mesmerizing, but as he settled into his job as senior pastor, some family issues surfaced within his family. Most of the issues were kept from many members, but the fact that he eventually separated from his wife became big news within the church, though all Ricky and the other children could do was speculate. The oldest daughter, Rachel, was a year older than Zariah, and the younger one, Melissa, was a year or two younger than Zariah.

Each summer during their middle school years, Ricky and his siblings were each sent to a Christian camp for one week every summer. Ricky went three times, the first two for horseback riding lessons, and the third time for tennis lessons. He enjoyed both, but was better at horseback riding. Tennis wasn't supposed to be a contact sport, but Ricky found a way. Just ask the tennis instructor during Ricky's one year spent taking tennis lessons. One day they were working on serves, and Ricky would cautiously serve the ball, sacrificing most of his power just to get it to land in the correct service area. Wanting to see Ricky put more force behind the serve, she challenged Ricky to show her his best serve, because she thought he was holding back his true potential. So at her suggestion, he threw caution to the wind and served it with all his might, without concern for accuracy. In spite of the force of the serve, it was an accurate serve, since it managed to drill the instructor right between the eyes. Like when David drilled Goliath in the forehead with a sling stone, the instructor also got knocked out cold by the force of Ricky's serve. That was the only time Ricky ever served the ball with all his might. That was also the extent of his tennis career.

Whenever a child within the church turned thirteen, they were expected to take confirmation classes. Ricky's class happened to be the first one pastor Fred was responsible for leading. They all went through a few weeks of classes at the church, with the final class sessions consisting of a confirmation retreat at the same Christian camp Ricky went to for horseback riding and tennis lessons. This time they were expected to attend spiritual growth classes with some of the ministry staff. Ricky skipped a couple of those classes, mostly because he would rather walk around on his own than sit through what he decided were boring classes. Since he wasn't restricted by having his parents around to dictate what he could or couldn't do, he took the time to explore his first taste of complete freedom without any fear of punishment. Opportunities like these also gave him the chance to be mischievous on occasion, in ways he never tried around the house. He once shared at one of the camps how he pulled the fire alarm on purpose, later convincing everyone he did it on accident.

After graduating his confirmation class, putting his little bit of mischievous rebellion behind him, he decided he wanted to try singing in the church choir. He wasn't a singing prodigy like his sister, but if he had to be there every week, he wanted to do more than just sit in the pew and do nothing. That was the ADD side of him coming out. There were two choirs, the senior choir and the junior choir. The senior choir was for adults, and the junior choir was for the students. Both choirs were led by the same family, mother and daughter. The mother, Mary, led the senior choir, while the daughter, Denise, was the junior choir director and organist during services. Mary was in her early sixties, and Denise was an attractive female in her late twenties. Zariah got along well with Denise because of their bond as females.

Ricky's main role within the choir was to join Mary's husband George, and another choir member named Fred, in providing the choir a sense of humor and laid back joviality. George, Fred and Ricky were their church's version of the Three Stooges, which was much needed to counteract Mary's rigid intensity to make sure everything was done right, and sounded flawless. The three of them were the heart of the tenor section, and while their antics were really amusing, when it came time to perform, they were all business. Ricky appreciated them, though he still couldn't share too much about his struggles with them, for fear of his parents finding out.

For that reason, Ricky also couldn't mention how he had a crush on Denise, even though she was married at the time. She drove a Trans Am with a personalized license plate, she liked the same hair band rock groups that Ricky and most other kids growing up in the 1980's did, she had a great figure with beautiful straight blonde hair, and looked so beautiful in her Sunday best every week. To a kid living in a backwoods town, it was like having a supermodel come play the organ at church every week! What kid wouldn't be smitten by a backwoods supermodel like Denise? There were one or two other female church members around his age that Ricky also thought were attractive, but given his missing testicle and resulting lack of confidence, he wasn't much interested in dating through church either. There are other reasons, which are the subject of the next chapter. The closest relationship he had was with a girl named Kim, who was the same age as Ricky. Like Ricky, she was also given similar intellectual expectations from the time she started kindergarten. She was one of a few people he got to know well, and spent a lot of time around, both in elementary school, church, and church choir. Because she was female, she grew more at a younger age, so she didn't have the same target on her back that scrawny Ricky did. Prior to high school they got along well, but as high school rolled around, their friendship seemed to drift apart. One particular incident between Ricky and Kim, which I discuss in the next chapter, had a profoundly negative effect on their friendship.

What I do know is that his time spent in church did little to provide him the spiritual maturity he longed for, to help him understand that his relationship with the God of the universe was as profound as it should have been to him. Even though he displayed the intellectual ability to display a strong willingness to understand more about Christianity, his relationship was always based solely on his intellectual ability to grasp the intellectual nature of the Bible. The social, emotional and spiritual understanding were never there, for all the reasons I mentioned. He did a good job of convincing everyone else there he had them, to avoid making his parents look bad. I say that because when he was in high school the church had a construction project, and after it was done they wanted a representative from each ministry group to take part in the groundbreaking. Ricky was chosen to represent the youth for the ribbon cutting ceremony. To Ricky, attending didn't really mean much to him. He was never all that interested in that type of fame, as it didn't come with a mentor, it didn't stop the abuse in school nor did it end the neglect at home, which were the only things in life he really wanted.

During the tail end of Ricky's senior year of high school, Ricky's grandfather Vernet – his dad's grandfather – was about to face his eternal future. Wanting the kids to remember their grandfather in a good way, the whole family went to visit him in the hospital. He was rarely conscious, and when he was, he didn't have much to say. Aside from the occasional trip growing up, to visit him at his rustic house in upstate New York, neither Ricky nor his siblings knew much about him, other than the fact that he and his second wife Florence were kind people with solid moral values, who had some fun activities for the kids to do on his property. Ricky especially enjoyed playing with his golf clubs. As with most other family get togethers, all the kids were segregated to hang out with each other, while the adults engaged in adult conversations that the kids were never permitted to be a part of. So when he was about to pass, the visits were really awkward for Ricky and his siblings, since they never related to their grandpa on any sort of adult level of conversation. Sensing a lack of maturity from all the kids, both parents agreed that bringing them back to see him in his dying condition was a bad idea. So Ricky's dad was the only one who often visited him after that initial awkward visit. A week or so later, Vernet did pass away. His second wife Florence also passed away around ten years later. Ricky got to inherit his grandpa's golf clubs, and all the kids, including his two cousins Julie and Michael, got to inherit some of his possessions. When Florence passed, she left a small trust fund for her five adopted grandchildren to enjoy.

Speaking of inheritance, some former members of the church who passed away a few years before Vernet and Florence, left a significant trust fund to the church in their will. Through the trust, a scholarship program was created for church members. In order to qualify for the scholarship, a member had to attend either New Brunswick Theological Seminary, Massachusetts Institute of Technology (MIT), or Hope College. It is a scholarship still available to any church member. Since Hope College was one of only two schools Ricky got accepted to (Penn State being the other), Ricky chose to fulfill his parents dream to be the first to graduate college by committing to attend there. According to the terms of the scholarship, it was to cover half of his tuition, but for Ricky's junior and senior year of college, the church decided to cut his scholarship to $2,500 per year, so as not to deplete the principal portion of the scholarship funds. This was a result of another member of the church who chose to attend MIT two years earlier. For those not familiar with MIT, it is a very expensive, very prestigious technical school, even today. This student was the older brother of Ricky's soccer teammate who led the state of New Jersey in scoring in seventh grade, and their family were also members of Ricky's church.

Now that I've painted an accurate picture of what church life was like for Ricky, I want to close out his religious experience by mentioning that when Ricky turned eighteen his high school education was nearing completion, and his time in the church was also about to end. That meant that he could now go forth and accomplish his parents' dream for Ricky's future, by being the first family member to graduate college. That also meant it was time for Ricky to keep his word and read the Bible cover to cover a second time. When he finished reading shortly before the end of his freshman year of college, he prayed for the wisdom Solomon had. Now there is an old fable which says: be careful what you wish for, you just might get it. Little did Ricky know how profound that prayer request would turn out to be many years later. The profound answer to that prayer will be how I – as narrator of Ricky's story – bring this book to a conclusion, the best way I know how. In the meantime, next I want to bring attention to the biggest social deficiency in Ricky's life: his understanding of how relationships with women work.

7

Addicted

"I'm feeling like a dog in heat
Barred indoors from the summer street
I locked the door to my own cell
And I lost the key
Bite my lip and close my eyes
Take me away to paradise
I'm so damn bored I'm going blind"

"Longview", Green Day

Personal addictions such as drugs, alcohol, cigarettes, or gambling all have well publicized organizations who utilize televised public service announcements to help people with those addictions. An addiction to pornography, however, rarely gets the same publicity, yet it's just as much of a negative addiction in society. Most sexual addicts / deviants, as with all the other forms mentioned above, get involved with their respective vice due to some deficiency in their upbringing. I guess that makes it the white elephant in a room full of external addictions.

Around the time Ricky turned twelve, he began to discover an interest in women. These days, he'd be considered a late bloomer, but when Ricky grew up, that was considered normal. Because he was expected to discover right from wrong, and how to navigate through life, entirely on his own, his social life was his to do with as he pleased. Doing so without a mentor meant that most of the things he did were not scrutinized by anyone (especially not his parents). There were a few exceptions: if it was illegal, it was something that ran contrary to the military-based family rules, or it somehow threatened anyone's life. Masturbation fit none of these categories, so he was simply left to continue doing so as a form of release from all the abuse in school, all the mentorship neglect at home, and all the expectations for success placed on him, while also being expected to do all this depending entirely on his own underdeveloped emotional understanding. This led to a severe social deficiency in his ability to relate to people, especially women. He was never given any opportunity to be open with his deepest feelings, because that's not what soldiers do. Because of his status as omega male at home and primary target for abuse in school, he chose to associate with all the misfits, who understood what it meant to not know how to relate to women. They also knew what it was like to be on the receiving end of abuse and/or neglect in life. The problem was that this social circle made dating anyone a near impossibility. The cute girls like Allyson were completely out of Ricky's league.

Adding to his sexual deficiencies was the fact that he never got the birds and the bees lecture, or any lecture on his sexuality, for that matter. Coupled with his low self-confidence from not being free to make any important decisions for himself or to openly express his feelings with anyone, he instead sought out ways to release his innermost urges privately, without ever having to discuss his fears or feelings with anyone else. It started one fall day in seventh grade middle school, when his eyes caught a glimpse of another cute blonde cheerleader in her cheerleader outfit. When he got home, he wanted to please himself by fantasizing about the thought of sexual relations with her. For most maladjusted kids, that's how it usually starts. It may seem innocent, but left unchecked, it can develop into something people like Ricky never intended. If you read about the type of person Ricky became in the beginning of the book, you'll understand how something so innocent can develop into something so dangerous. I'll discuss this reality later in the chapter.

Since Ricky never had any guidance on how to develop interpersonal social skills with women, as I mentioned in previous chapters, he found comfort by escaping into the fantasy world of masturbation. This escape led him to solely base his interest in females based on their physical attributes. The emotional and / or spiritual aspects of being able to relate to women was something Ricky was never taught, and never had anything in the way of experience to guide his understanding either. For the most part, Ricky simply avoided dating relationships, since he imagined it leading to nothing but emotional pain.

Having a missing testicle added another powerful element of fear in his life regarding dating. In Ricky's eyes, the merciless ridicule that awaited him should anyone ever find that out, led Ricky to believe he'd receive a dating death sentence from women everywhere. He already dealt with the ridicule of being pointed at every time he had to adjust himself in gym class, and imagined it would be much worse if his secret got out through a woman. That haunting scenario led Ricky to withdraw further and further into his masturbation fantasy life. Unfortunately, the decision by Ricky's parents not to mentor and teach him right from wrong in this area, only led him further down this road than I ever wanted him to go. They stood by and let him find escape in his fantasy world of masturbating anytime he wanted, without any of the pain or relational commitment involved with dating.

As for what this can do to a person mentally and emotionally, I bring light to the issue by discussing the influence masturbation had on two other people who are well remembered in this nation's history. The first is David Berkowitz, known to most people as the notorious "Son of Sam" killer. Like Ricky, Berkowitz also had a troubled childhood. Dr. James Dobson, from his time with Focus on the Family, conducted an interview with Berkowitz, and said this about Berkowitz:

> "He was a loner. He felt rejected by his birth mother. His adopted birth mother died. Isolated on the street. You end up seeing this pattern of being deeply wounded as a child, and pulling into your own shell, and becoming more strange as time goes on. Isolation rots the mind." [8]

All of these attributes led both Ricky and Berkowitz to develop an unnatural desire for women. They developed a view of

---

8 "Son of Sam", Dr. James Dobson Interview with David Berkowitz, March 2004, Focus on the Family.

most people – women in particular – as little more than physical objects, or pawns in a game where they each became the center of a fantasy world they could retreat into any time they wanted. In his interview with Dr. Dobson, Berkowitz describes his masturbation habit this way:

> "When I was a teenager, I remember seeing pornographic movies for the first time, and I was fascinated by that. When I went into the service, there was pornography all over the place, because I think service personnel are probably the biggest purchasers of pornographic stuff, you know the Penthouses, the Playboys, the Hustlers, they were all over the place. So I was reading them constantly, as part of, just the boredom, you're there on the post, you have nothing to do, no place to go, you spend hours and hours just reading this pornographic literature. I developed an addiction to it, I found it fascinating." [9]

As Berkowitz's addiction to pornography grew, in much the same way it did for Ricky, he saw women as nothing more than objects of flesh without any feeling. This dehumanization was his motivation to become the infamous serial killer of women in New York City. As you read in Chapter 1, this dehumanization of women eerily turned Ricky into a similar psychopath. As to how masturbation affects the person growing more addicted to it over time, Berkowitz describes it this way:

> "In a sense, [pornography] caused me to devalue the lives of other people somewhat. ... It was, at the time, since I didn't have a girlfriend, I worked the night shift,

---

9   "Son of Sam", ibid.

I worked all these different jobs with all these weird hours, night hours, I didn't have much of a social life, I really wanted to find a girlfriend, but I used to just resort to fantasies with that stuff ... I know that it [pornography and masturbation] ... probably hardened my heart in many ways."[10]

The second person, fellow serial killer Ted Bundy, wanted others to hear him talk about his addiction to pornography to discourage people from doing it. On the day before his execution, also in an interview with Dr. James Dobson, Bundy said this about his addiction to pornography:

"This [pornography] is something, I think, I want to emphasize. The most damaging kinds of pornography, and again, I'm talking from personal experience. Hard, real personal experience. The most damaging kinds of pornography are those that involve violence, and sexual violence. Because the wedding of those two forces, as I only know all too well, brings about behavior that is just too terrible to describe."

"I was essentially a normal person, I had good friends, I lived a normal life, except for this one small but very potent, and very destructive segment of it, I kept very secret and very close to myself and didn't let anyone know about it."

"In the beginning, it fuels this kind of thought process. Then, at a certain time, it's instrumental in [how it] crystallizes, making it into something which is almost like a

---

10   "Son of Sam", ibid.

separate entity inside. At that point you're at the verge, I was at the verge, of acting out those kind of thoughts."

"It [his addiction to pornography] happened in stages, gradually. It doesn't necessarily, not to me at least, happen overnight. My experience with say, pornography, generally, but with pornography that deals on a violent level with sexuality, is that once you become addicted to it, and I look at this as a kind of addiction. Like other kinds of addiction, it would keep looking for more potent, more explicit, more graphic kinds of material. Like an addiction, you keep craving something which is harder, something which gives you a greater sense of excitement, until you reach the point where the pornography only goes so far. You reach that jumping off point where you begin to wonder if maybe, actually doing it, will give you that which is beyond just reading about it or looking at it."

Bundy concluded his thoughts by saying this:

"I've lived in prison for a long time now. I've met a lot of men [here in prison] who are motivated to commit violence just like me. Without exception, every one of them was deeply involved in pornography ... Deeply influenced and consumed by an addiction to pornography ... The FBI's own study on serial homicide shows that the most common interest among serial killers is pornography." [11]

---

[11] "Fatal Addiction", Dr. James Dobson Interview with Ted Bundy, January 23, 1989. https://www.youtube.com/watch?v=08dpnn0cd10. By request of the Bundy family, the interview is no longer one Dr. Dobson's ministry is permitted to release. I found the interview itself at the Youtube link listed instead, though there is no guarantee the link will be available for public viewing in the future.

Like Ricky, neither Bundy nor Berkowitz had a mentor to guide them. They also shared a lack of knowledge how to treat a woman as anything more than an object to be fantasized over. In the same way, masturbation was a natural release for Ricky to deal with his lack of emotional maturity / mentorship / sex education. Like Bundy, Ricky started experimenting with it in middle school, gradually sinking deeper into that world as he got older. I wish I had been able to be more of an influence on Ricky in this area. If I had, I might have been able to convince him it was wrong for him to go down this path, based on all the negative consequences that Berkowitz spoke of. Instead, I chose to leave that decision up to his parents to teach him right from wrong in this area. While his parents did give him effective guidance in some areas of his life, guidance on the dangers of masturbation, as with all other lessons on sexuality, were lessons Ricky never received.

As Ricky got to high school, thanks to this complete lack of guidance, his unchecked fantasy masturbation addiction got worse, exactly the way Bundy described. Every Sunday he looked forward to watching wrestling after church. As I discuss in more detail in the next chapter, professional wrestling also appealed to Ricky's non-sexual fantasy life. Thanks to video recording, he could tape and later watch episodes anytime he wanted. Since females rarely wrestled, what few females that appeared on TV back then, usually dressed up in very beautiful, and very expensive outfits. Ricky's clear favorite was Miss Elizabeth, as she always looked so glamorous dressed in her Sunday best on television, which made her someone Ricky enjoyed fantasizing about, even if she was taken. On the show Price is Right, Barker's Beauties were equally erotic, since their sole purpose on the show was to appeal to male sexuality while promoting whatever products were being given away as prizes. According to Ricky, all of them were really good at appealing to his fantasy life. Those were just a few of the more prominent TV females he fantasized regularly towards, but there were thousands of others he could fantasize about on TV. He also fantasized about most of the women in school, especially when they dressed up in revealing outfits that showcased their best body parts. Over time, Ricky enjoyed coming home to fantasize about his attractive classmates every day after school. He went so far as to create his own fantasy ranking system, based on which ones he was most attracted to. He didn't know how to relate to them, he was never taught anything about how to understand them, and he was never given any understanding that having an opportunity to learn otherwise was in any way beneficial. As a result, he simply retreated further and further into his sexual fantasy world of soft-core pornography, without any efforts by anyone in his life to attempt to stop or correct his socially deviant behavior.

Outside the home, Ricky never openly attempted to manifest his deviant behavior with women, mostly because he knew he would get physically beat up by that specific female's boyfriend, along with his (and her) entire circle of friends, as well as become even more of an outcast worthy of additional abuse, much worse than what he already dealt with.

There were, however, two times when this fantasy life manifested itself negatively in Ricky's reality. The first was the day when his longtime friend Kim dressed up for school, in a way that was sexually inviting to Ricky. She sat next to him on the bus that day. So he got to see her the whole time sitting there next to him looking really beautiful in her revealing outfit. Now

I already mentioned the occasional blackout due to ADD, and this was clearly the most embarrassing. Right there on the bus, while staring at Kim's body, he blacked out. When he regained consciousness around a minute or two later, everyone was looking at him and commenting how he was staring at her body. This certainly changed the entire dynamic of his relationship with Kim, both in church choir and with everyone else at school. When your deficiencies are on full display for everyone to gossip about, the gossip spreads faster than a raging wildfire.

Ironically, the other time his perverted sexual fantasy life manifested itself was in church. One day he was chatting with Denise while she played the closing music to end the service. While she was often out of view behind the organ, Ricky always liked to appreciate how good she looked. Once he enjoyed it a little too much, going so far as to actually touch her beautiful figure after the services as she played the closing song one week. When she slid away, he resumed contact with her. It made her feel extremely awkward, but Ricky didn't care. For him, this was the only way he knew how to express his deepest emotions with others, since he had never been taught any healthy ways to express himself, especially with females. This deviant form of sexual release was one which he was allowed to pursue unchecked for years after that fateful day when he first spotted that cute cheerleader in seventh grade.

Now that I've touched on all the negative influences that he had to deal with that led Ricky to develop into the psychopath he became, I want to discuss the other positive influence in his life worth discussing during high school. This activity was one his parents allowed him to continue to participate in, even with his bad grades. The more he got involved, the more he developed leadership skills and positive values in his life – important life lessons Ricky never learned at home, school or at church, since church was mostly about having fun and learning Bible stories. Ricky especially enjoyed this activity because it was the one area in his life where he could be who he wanted to be by participating in something without his parents' overbearing influence on everything he said or did, where there was no abuse or neglect, and where punishment was fully designed to help teach him to strive to constructively make something of himself. It is this activity that I will discuss in the next chapter.

8

Hero

"I'm just a step away, I'm just a breath away
Losin' my faith today, fallin' off the edge today
I am just a man, not superhuman
I'm not superhuman ... Someone save me from the hate
I need a hero, to save my life"

"Hero", Skillet

Six years after Grandpa John passed away, Ricky finally found people he could look up to that would give him the guidance to become the type of person he should be. I'm referring to the good guys, or hero wannabes Ricky watched on TV every weekend. Most people know them as professional wrestlers. When Ricky was about twelve, Hulk Hogan was just establishing himself as the ideal role model for Ricky. With his mantra of, "To all my little Hulkamaniacs, say your prayers, take your vitamins and you will never go wrong" [12], along with the idea of

---

12 https://www.azquotes.com/author/6807-Hulk_Hogan

overcoming his opposition by physically defeating them in the wrestling ring, everything professional wrestling represented gave Ricky the hope that he too could one day physically overcome the same abuse he dealt with at school, just like the Hulkster! The only problem was there was no personal mentorship, just a generic concept of right vs. wrong as played out in and around wrestling arenas. Ricky also saw this as an opportunity to grow in his faith (and possibly physically look just like the Hulkster one day), since he believed the Hulkster was obviously a Christian for promoting prayers to the "Big Man Upstairs". The only difference was that unlike the Hulkster, Ricky wasn't able to exclaim truthfully, "God created the Heavens, he created the earth! He created all the Hulkamaniacs! Then, he created a set of twenty-four-inch pythons, brother!" [13] Ricky's pythons, however, were more like baby garter snakes, barely measuring six inches – on a good day!

Now yes, I've heard many people parrot how wrestling is fake. So are over 98% of the TV shows and movies that have been made in the last seventy years, and most Americans spend more hours watching them than Ricky spent watching wrestling. Wrestlers are actors just like movie stars, the only difference being that with wrestlers, their stage is the area in and around a wrestling ring. However, because of Ricky's lack of social maturity as a teenager, he believed it was real. Believing it was real helped Ricky find someone to look up to, since no one else stepped up to fill the role of mentor after Grandpa John passed away. Now while it may be acceptable to tell an adult that it's fake, telling a child that is a bad idea, for much the same reason it would be a bad idea to tell a child Santa Claus isn't real.

---

13 https://quotereel.com/hulk-hogan-quotes/

Many of today's youth also need role models to look up to, and Ricky's lone role models in life, were the professional wrestlers who fought for good on TV every week. He always looked forward to watching, because the only genuine inspiration he got in life came from watching the good wrestlers defeat those who stood for what was wrong. Now his understanding of good and evil was also greatly stunted, in large part due to his obvious lack of mentorship. The disciplinary, fear-based family environment he lived in at home and in church, and the hell he endured at school, made openly trusting any real person very difficult. So the professional wrestlers were the only people Ricky could look up to for guidance and mentorship in life.

As for the other good decision Ricky's parents made, it was their decision to have Ricky and Robby join the Cub / Boy Scouts. Given Ricky's militaristic upbringing, this was an ideal fit for the disciplinary lifestyle Ricky was accustomed to. It also helped Ricky become more well-rounded and adept at lots of different life skills. Cub Scouts was fairly easy for Ricky, as most of the activities were intellectually based. They were also inside a school, this time with other leaders present who cared enough to ensure there was no abuse between scouts. When Robby joined a year later, this was one of the few areas where Robby had to rely on Ricky for guidance and leadership. In trailblazer fashion, Ricky did what he could to help Robby keep up. When they each turned eleven, they both graduated to Boy Scouts.

There were three troops in town, two that were sponsored by other churches. One was at an Episcopal church, one was at a Catholic church, and the third was sponsored by the local American Legion post. As a former veteran, of course their dad chose the one sponsored by the American Legion. It was a much easier transition for Ricky, and when Robby again followed Ricky's footsteps a year later, Ricky was finally able to effectively fulfill his responsibility as trailblazer. The council leadership structure made that possible for a change – a very refreshing change for Ricky. At first the troop was run by the town hardware store owner, who later became town mayor. The only reason he led the troop was because he wanted to "donate" all his old camping equipment for a tax deduction. He may have been a good hardware store owner, and a decent mayor, but he was a crappy Scoutmaster, according to Ricky. The tents he donated were in crappy condition, and weren't very effective at keeping the boys safe from inclement weather. As Scoutmaster, campouts were simply a relaxing weekend away from the stress of being a dad and a hardware store owner. At least that's what Ricky thought, given how this Scoutmaster never did anything for the scouts. There was no rank advancement, well not quite. He did teach everyone in the troop about basket weaving and cooking. He only taught basket weaving since selling the basket supplies helped him make a small profit for his hardware store. He taught cooking because he expected the kids to do all his cooking and dish washing each campout, to give him a break from having to do it himself. Other than that, he expected Jimi (then the Senior Patrol leader – the same Jimi that was the oldest of the three Ice brothers from Ricky's neighborhood) to teach the rest of the troop first aid, mainly in case anyone got hurt during the campout. This lack of leadership was Robby's sign that his alpha male mentality would be able to help assume control within the troop, since this Scoutmaster had no desire to do anything for the kids. So Robby and the two older Ice boys took charge, as they were the alpha males among the troop. Ricky had little choice but to go along with their leadership. Given how close knit the relationship was between his family and the Ice boys, going along with the mischief was one of two options, and I discuss the alternative below.

They only camped outdoors in tents during the spring, summer and fall, and in cabins during the winter. Each cabin clearly had enough room for the entire troop and the heat worked a little too well. So sleeping in a bunk usually meant not needing to use a sleeping bag. Except for those few occasions where they cooked, cleaned and weaved baskets, the troop spent the rest of their daylight conducting recon to learn where all the other troops were staying. At night they would return to their least favorite other troop campsite(s), to knock down their tents and sabotage their supplies that night, when cabins weren't used. It was the one thing the troop was known for, which is what happens when leadership isn't actively invested in the scouts. Anyone who didn't go along with the kids' mischievous ways, or who didn't carry their weight cooking or cleaning, received the most grueling form of punishment that they could come up with. Ricky referred to it as the "sticky burn", and anyone who woke up from it once, knew better than to endure it a second time.

The sticky burn consisted of two ingredients. The first one was marshmallows placed inside another scout's underwear while they slept. The mini-marshmallows were preferred as they weren't as easily felt when carefully placed in another scout's underwear. They could even be poured in, straight from the bag, with little effort. They also melted faster and spread out quicker, to make sure the underwear couldn't easily be removed. When a campout was approaching, Ricky and Robby and the two Ice boys always made sure that there was always enough hot chocolate and marshmallows. What mom wouldn't make sure their little camper had hot chocolate and marshmallows on a campout? Since Jimi was the Senior Patrol Leader, he had 24-7 access to the food supplies, which he could easily access anytime he wanted to send a message to another scout.

The other key ingredient in the "sticky burn" was toothpaste. This too was something all moms had to make sure their little camper always had as part of their camping supplies. If you've ever felt that tingly sensation you get when brushing your teeth, imagine how much stronger the tingly sensation would be when applied to the area around a boy's private parts. The preferred toothpaste of choice was always AquaFresh, as it had three separate ingredients in it, which according to the boys' logic, meant three different burning sensations, once it fully did its work to the unsuspecting sleeping camper.

The other necessity was a small forked stick, so that contact with the skin / underwear movement would be minimal and less likely to be noticed by a sleeping scout. None of them wanted to touch another scout's dirty underwear anyway. They all preferred if a scout slept on his stomach, as the victim was less likely to wake up, and they could squeeze the toothpaste deep into the person's buttcrack. If they slept on their back, the area around the testicles was usually more painful, but also more difficult to pull off without waking up the victim. If the victim slept on either side, they had their choice of front or back, and they often chose both sides. Once in place, Ricky, Robby and the two older Ice boys crept back to their bunks, waiting patiently for the screaming to begin. They often laughed quietly while pretending to sleep after they finished. Then it was just a question of waiting until the screaming started as the victim quickly made his way to the latrine to stop the burning. If the scouts stayed in tents, it was more difficult to sneak into other tents to apply the sticky burn, but still possible. If they stayed in a cabin, there was no difficulty whatsoever zeroing in on their target.

Once all scouts within the troop were on board with the troop mentality, thanks to the threat of a(nother) sticky burn, they could all focus on causing mischief with other troops. It didn't really matter which troop, though the other two rival troops from town were preferred, particularly the Catholic church troop, whom Ricky's troop considered their arch-rival troop. They had the most scouts and won most of the scouting events – Klondike Derby, best troop, etc. Sabotaging other troops from outside their hometown was also fun, too, just to be fair to everyone. The recon team always went out with the mission of determining who was camping at which campsite. Of course, that also meant that other troops would be seeking revenge, so guarding their own equipment was equally important. Their favorite activity was pulling up the tent poles, so as to collapse the tents while the other troop's scouts slept at night. Having a scoutmaster who didn't really care made it all the more fun! If they stayed in cabins, they were limited to the amount of mischief they could inflict on other troops. Breaking into cabins at night meant being outnumbered and unable to escape if they were discovered.

Now if you're thinking like I and most parents would, you'd ask what did they do to earn merit badges and rank advancement? Aside from basket weaving, cooking and first aid, nothing. They did focus on the basics, so that most everyone did manage to earn their first rank, which was the rank of Tenderfoot. Beyond that, the motivation was left entirely up to the scouts. With Jimi as leader, and Jeff, Ricky and Robby as his three sergeants-at-arms, all the others didn't have a choice but to fall in line with their mischievous ways.

Around the time Ricky turned fourteen, the troop had a change in scoutmasters. Replacing the hardware store owner was a younger guy in his mid-twenties who happened to live near the hardware store owner. With this new scoutmaster meant lots of changes. Gone were the days of rebellious mischief. Replacing it was an atmosphere of responsibility and dedication. Robby, being the mischievous alpha male, eventually got frustrated with the direction the troop was heading under the new scoutmaster, so he quit. The primary factor in his decision was how this new environment meant Ricky's intellect made him the alpha male of the troop. Robby wasn't going to be part of allowing someone else to be the alpha male, *especially* when the alpha male was now going to be his own brother. A few other neighborhood kids quit along with Robby, and this was also around the time the Ice family left New Jersey for California. Ricky, on the other hand, embraced the change. For some reason he saw something in the new scoutmaster, a new start with the mentor he'd longed for since Grandpa John passed away. As Ricky bought into the new scoutmaster's plan, it really brought out the best in Ricky. His insights proved correct here, for he did finally receive the blessing of having a mentor he could turn to for helping him develop his own personality, his own gifts, and to do so in a reward / punishment environment, where everyone was given an equal chance to succeed. Because of Ricky's intellect, his knowledge made him someone everyone else looked up to for a refreshing change. This helped him to finally begin the process of learning how to become the person he always wanted to develop into

— the person he was never allowed to become at home or at school — himself!

Of course Ricky was far behind the rank advancement guidelines expected of most scouts his age. By age 14, most scouts would have earned their First Class rank (the third of six ranks for those unfamiliar with Boy Scouts), with the really motivated scouts already earning Star (fourth of six) rank by fourteen. Prior to the change in scoutmasters, as I've already illustrated, none of the scouts were very motivated. Since Ricky was still a Tenderfoot (first of six), he had lots of work to do to catch up. Even becoming an Eagle Scout was still possible, given Ricky's rank at age 14, but it would be quite a challenge for him to do it. He was certainly intelligent enough to make it happen. Now that he finally had someone in his life to challenge him to make something of himself, he was willing to try.

Before I get into how far Ricky advanced, I wanted to talk about his scoutmaster. His name was Roy, and like the hardware store owner, Roy also lived in one of the flood prone areas on the east side of town, just north of the tracks. Because of the challenges the neighborhood flooding caused, his house was certainly no palace. But then again, for those who lived in those parts of town, adversity brought all sorts of challenges, some which went way beyond the flooding. For Roy, his father was often very physically abusive towards him. While Ricky was never physically abused himself, he certainly understood what it felt like to fear one's father. That drill sergeant story still reminded him what that was like, even if Ricky never physically felt the pain Roy felt.

Like Ricky, Roy also grew up in a church environment, also

because his parents made him go. The main difference was that Ricky had to go every week. Roy's parents weren't as strict as Ricky's parents. For that reason, Roy's spiritual maturity was less developed than Ricky's. That's not to say that Roy was less of a person than Ricky, but having spoken to both of them, I knew deep down Ricky had the intellectual ability to grasp the spiritual aspects of life in ways few were able to. That was why I was so interested in maintaining a close relationship with Ricky.

Maybe it was Roy's desire not to be like his father that motivated him to make a difference in other people's lives. Maybe he just wanted to live out his faith by helping others. Regardless of the reason, his influence in Ricky's life, along with the others who remained in the troop, led Ricky to fully embrace the changes Roy instituted, all of which had both an immediate and a lasting positive influence on the boys.

If a scout did something wrong, pushups or sit-ups were the usual form of punishment. It helped the scouts in two ways. First, it served to motivate them to do what was right according to the Scout Oath and Law. Second, it helped increase their level of physical fitness. Both were definitely needed in Ricky's life. Of course, there was positive reinforcement for the scouts who did the right thing too. That was something Ricky never experienced at home or in school, which was the biggest reason he embraced the change.

With this highly effective system of rewards and punishments in place, each scout better understood what was expected of him. As the first few months with Roy as Scoutmaster unfolded, Ricky displayed the strongest willingness to buy into the system. Once the scouts that remained got fully acclimated to the changes brought about by Roy, it was time to make the transition to allow the scouts the opportunity to learn how to lead each other – in a constructive manner! That scout led leadership structure has always been something the Boy Scouts encourages their scouts to learn and embody. Because Roy saw in Ricky the most potential for leadership, he was chosen to be the first one to handle the primary leadership responsibility of Senior Patrol Leader. It was a brand new challenge for Ricky, and he had some apprehension at first. Most who are thrust into leadership for the first time usually do. Given his desire and his respect for his new mentor, he didn't just succeed, he excelled in his new role.

With the days of sticky burn, pulling up tent stakes of other troops, and other assorted mischief now little more than a memory, Ricky got to work leading and achieving the potential no one else ever gave him the opportunity or the guidance to instill in himself. And to think there was a time when his parents also considered preventing him from participating in Boy Scouts, in addition to not playing sports, due to his bad grades. Looking back on his time in Scouting, Ricky recalled how beneficial it was when Robby quit. Ricky's dad still only had a strong bond with Robby, and when Robby quit, his dad stopped showing interest as well. Had Robby stayed their dad may have signed on as a leader, spending more time helping Robby develop into a leader, leaving Ricky to be forced to again walk in Robby's footsteps, stunting his own growth as a leader. Having an outlet where he could develop on his own, free from his parents' influence, with a mentor that was willing to give him all the responsibility, meant everything to Ricky. It was certainly better than the second-hand, leftover scraps he was forced to accept at home and at school.

For the next 3+ years, Monday night scout meetings became the highlight of Ricky's week. Summer camps were great too, as they gave him the freedom to pursue his intellectual passion for learning on his own, without any of the pressure of displeasing his parents. As a result, in only 3+ years, Ricky earned all the educational requirements for earning Eagle Scout. The only thing that kept him from becoming an Eagle Scout were the two service projects he had to complete for Life and Eagle Ranks, neither of which he was able to coordinate and complete prior to turning 18 years old – the final day for eligibility in the Boy Scouts. So his Scouting career officially ended with him only going as far as Star rank.

Here Ricky also learned how to work together with, and motivate others, to succeed at the two annual troop competitions – the Klondike Derby and the School Derby. The Klondike Derby meant having to break out the sled and take turns pulling it like the sled dogs do in the Iditarod race. With the Boy Scouts, the troops were also required to stop at certain checkpoints and perform various skills taught in the Boy Scouts. It was never something the troop did well in, as none of the kids were very big, and aside from Ricky, not as old, or as smart. The School Derby, on the other hand, was more appealing. Held on the very same middle school gymnasium that served as the source of ridicule for always adjusting himself during gym class, School Derby served as the place where the troop had a fighting chance to win. One event in particular was always the most exhilarating for Ricky's troop. It was the one event they were always heavy favorites to win, having always won every year, and no other troop ever challenged their dominance in this event – none even came close. I'm talking about the ten-scout pyramid. In this event, when the assigned judge shouted go, all ten Scouts had to run like cheetahs being chased by lions, from one sideline of the basketball court to the other. When they crossed the other sideline, the bottom four had to drop to their hands and knees in a straight line, and get set quickly so the second row of three following immediately behind them could climb up and properly position their knees and hands on their shoulders and back, and so on with the remaining three. In the meantime, each scout already in position had to keep his body rigidly straight while supporting the weight of the scouts above him without collapsing from the strain of the extra weight on their backs. The longer it took, the harder the strain for the scouts on the bottom to maintain the weight above them. In spite of his size, Ricky was one of the larger scouts in the troop, which meant always being one of the four on the bottom. This was also the only time Robby came back to the troop, as his size and strength were also needed as part of the bottom four of the pyramid. When the scout on top was situated, using only his knees for balance, he had to hold the scout salute for three seconds while announcing his troop # to the judges. Unlike other troops, Ricky's troop – Troop 70 – never ever fell or collapsed due to muscle fatigue. One year however, the boys were extremely disappointed with their performance. They still won easily, that wasn't the disappointing part. They were disappointed because it was the first – and only – time it took them over ten seconds to complete the pyramid. Apparently the scout on top that year hesitated for a brief second before regaining his balance in order to salute, ruining their chance to maintain their flawless execution by finishing in under ten seconds. As a result, Ricky always cherished the ten-scout pyramid as it was his moment to experience the thrill of victory, both individually and as the leader of a unified team.

But the story doesn't end there. After Ricky completed his time in the troop and went off to college, the environment in the troop slowly changed. None of the other kids developed the same bond with Roy that Ricky did, so there wasn't any standout leader to replace him. As a result, this also had an effect on Roy's leadership. The news of the decline of the troop broke Ricky's heart, when he first heard. After Ricky left, Roy began sexually molesting some of the other scouts. As word got out around town, Roy's reputation as both a leader and as a person was ruined. Unfortunately, the rumors circulated that Ricky was one of his victims as well, and those rumors still exist to this day, even in the minds of Ricky's own parents, but no one ever believed Ricky when he stated numerous times that Roy never attempted to sexually molest him. Aside from fulfilling his role as the defacto leader of the troop, Ricky still had the same underdeveloped heart and spirit he always had at home, with the same fear of what his dad might do if he considered engaging in any sexual behavior with another man. Failing to live up to the soldier standard his dad emblazoned – with MUCH fear – into the body that was clearly inferior to his dad's, meant a much greater punishment – one even Roy knew not to expose Ricky to. Since Roy had met Ricky's father on a few occasions, Roy was almost as afraid of Ricky's father as Ricky was. The way I see it, Roy knew that doing anything to Ricky meant paternal punishment similar to what Roy endured at home. To keep Ricky from also enduring that, he avoided any interactions that would lead Ricky to be punished at home.

Roy probably also knew Ricky already had enough clouds hanging over his life: the heavy burden of his parents' expectations of success; spending most of his life with no personal role model; all the abuse from classmates; having no understanding of male / female relationships (and sexually molesting him would have only emotionally stunted him even more, which Roy likely understood); finding release in the fantasy worlds of role-playing games, professional wrestling and masturbation; and now having to attend college knowing that your only personal role model was an ephebophiliac (an adult who likes to molest children between the ages of fifteen to nineteen). But all these burdens were ones Ricky was forced to carry with him as he began the world of college as a young adult, seven hundred and fifty miles from home.

9

Crash & Burn

> "Hey man, get out of my face
> I deal with my problems at my own pace
> With your-screwed down, anti-human views
> Deal with the pressures by playing the blues
> If you wanna' live life on your own terms
> You gotta be willing to crash and burn"
>
> "Primal Scream", Motley Crue

Once Ricky finally managed to graduate high school – despite his lack of motivation due to all the events that largely destroyed his desire to succeed, and hindered his ability to focus – he spent his final summer with his family on their one month cross-country trip in the family van towing a pop-up camper. Though at times it resembled National Lampoon's vacation, Ricky did enjoy himself as most of the sites were ones worth visiting. I refer to camping in the Poconos / aquatic events along the Delaware River, taking a tour of the football hall of Fame in

Canton, OH, visiting the college he was about to begin attending that fall, staying with his step aunt (Ricky's mom's brother's ex-wife) in Minneapolis while visiting the Minneapolis Zoo (where she worked), visiting Mount Rushmore on 4th of July for their 100th anniversary celebration, Yellowstone Park, successfully dealing with some extremely challenging horseback riding in Cody, Wyoming (which all the males of the family thoroughly enjoyed, according to Ricky), touring a small casino city complex carved out of rocks in Colorado, Bryce Canyon, Grand Teton Mountains, Grand Canyon – where the majority of their stay was during the annual downpour, which started literally less than ten minutes after they arrived to the campsite. After Grand Canyon the boring return leg of the trip led them back through New Mexico, a dingy run down hotel in Dallas, Texas where the bugs were everywhere and the cockroaches were bigger than a human finger. No wonder the family hated the Cowboys! After that they drove through Arkansas, followed by the Blue Ridge and Appalachian mountains before returning home. Once home from the semi-enjoyable trip, Ricky and Robby spent the rest of that final summer working with their dad at the sign making shop that his dad was an electrical installer for.

While working with his dad's company, one day Ricky had a conversation with one of their co-workers, an Italian guy who painted a lot of the signs that the company created. Ricky believed the guy's name was Paul, but that's not relevant. The conversation was relevant because this was the second time Ricky showed signs of a psychotic side, like he did with his classmate Andre. Since his dad and brother were out of the shop on an installation, he didn't have to worry about either of them hearing his conversation, so he spoke from his heart.

That day Ricky told of his thirst for revenge against all the kids in high school that unmercifully taunted and belittled him because of the myriad of ways in which he was made to feel inferior. Given Ricky's underdeveloped heart, he managed to convince himself that when he had the resources and the physical ability to exact revenge, doing so would make him feel better, and make all the pain go away. Paul, being the super nice guy that everybody liked, tried to convince him otherwise, but his words didn't have any effect on Ricky.

Now Ricky clearly possessed the intellectual capacity to succeed in both high school and college. His parents frequently talked about his intellectual gifts. However, aside from what little he learned in Boy Scouts, Ricky had very little in the way of possessing the maturity to effectively function with the emotional, spiritual, or social skills needed to guide his intellect. Courtesy of Roy's disgrace after Ricky left for college, even his status as Ricky's mentor was heavily questioned. Most kids who go down this path become nerds, completely dysfunctional when it comes to understanding interpersonal relationships with any non-nerds. Now faced with the daunting task of surviving on his own in college, he quickly realized he needed all those skills – skills he didn't have – to survive as an adult for the rest of his life. One of the few good decisions he did make starting out in his adult life was to decide to pursue a bachelor's degree in Computer Science. Since he fit the description of a wimpy nerd, he figured continuing down this road to become a computer programmer was a natural fit for an anti-social loser like him. He didn't know what that entailed, just that working with computers was something the intellectual-only nerd in him could grasp, or so he thought.

As he got adjusted to his pursuit of this degree, outside of the classroom, his nerd lifestyle meant more of the same abuse, only this time he had nowhere to go for refuge, since his own roommate, affectionately known as "fos" (which stands for full of s*&%), was one of his abusers. This allowed his abusers unlimited access into an even greater part of Ricky's life there on the third floor of the dorm. Ricky recounts often returning to his room only to regularly find shaving cream in his bed, shampoo in the bags of chips he often snacked on, along with the usual physical and verbal abuse he'd grown accustomed to in high school. He did his best to pretend not to let it get to him, but deep down he still hated it, and harbored the same thoughts of one day exacting revenge, only now he had more targets to include in his quest. The only difference was that since the guys from the third floor had greater access into his life, they deserved a greater dose of revenge. In Ricky's mind, he'd make sure they one day received their full share of revenge as well.

In spite of the abuse, Ricky did discover he had the freedom to experience the outside world without any of the burdensome expectations of being the success story his parents always dreamed he would be. While he still harbored thoughts of revenge in his heart, he did look for opportunities to grow and explore life outside both his dorm and the classroom, without the restrictive micromanagement by his parents prior to college. Knowing it helped him find freedom from his abusers made his unfettered exploration of the world around him a lot more exciting. Ricky tried his hand at photography for the school yearbook, 1980's movie marathons with some of the dorm's second floor misfits he liked hanging out with, pickup basketball every day at noon with other students and professors, and weekly Fellowship of Christian Athletes meetings every Monday night (even if he wasn't much of an athlete anymore, not that he ever was to begin with). He was so excited to discover all these new experiences he didn't even mind that others were getting credit for most of his yearbook photos.

His excitement also motivated him to try out for the college baseball team his freshman year. Ricky still envisioned himself as a successful athlete that would one day make his dad proud, though he soon found out that the guys he was trying out alongside of were in much better baseball shape than Ricky was. Unlike them, Ricky hadn't played much in high school, nor was he recruited to play. He discovered really quickly that he was not physically capable of playing with his teammates. This became most evident when Ricky discovered he couldn't even come close to contacting a 90+ mile-per-hour fastball, as he'd never faced such a challenge before. His only hit came after he dejectedly said to the catcher from the other team, "another at bat, another strikeout." The catcher must have had sympathy on Ricky, because the pitcher threw Ricky a meatball to hit (a meatball is the baseball term for a pitch easy enough for anyone to hit). Well Ricky did manage to make contact with the pitch in that meaningless fall scrimmage game, and the ball barely left the infield for his only college hit.

His excitement was short lived. Later that fall, part of their fall conditioning involved throwing drills. Since Ricky wanted to play outfield, the conditioning drills consisted of throwing diagonally across two basketball courts for the better part of two hours a day, six days a week, for three straight weeks. As a result of his shoulder not being trained to handle that rigorous level of exercise, Ricky so overworked his throwing shoulder, that his ability to throw a baseball was severely limited from that point on. In spite of all the pain, in typical Ricky fashion, he continued to give his all on the field, regardless of how he felt.

Unfortunately, his all wasn't enough, as he simply wasn't skilled enough to make the team. When he got cut, he finished with a career batting average of .143 (or 1-7 for you statisticians out there), largely thanks to the generosity of that one opposing team's catcher. Because he enjoyed the game, and because he still wanted to stay involved with the team, he volunteered to assist the team by serving as the team manager. This is the polite version of a role as coach's errand boy / gopher. Ricky did so happily, as it kept him involved in the game he enjoyed, thinking maybe he'd make the team in the future, the same way Michael Jordan did after being cut from his high school basketball team.

Prior to his adventures with the baseball team, and his desire to explore new adventures once free from his parents' military upbringing, he also discovered alcoholic drinking parties every weekend. Considering how much pressure his parents placed on him to have that bright future open only to college graduates, and to be the first family member to honor their dreams by graduating college (which they never did), they were somehow willing to accept the fact that he often spent his weekends partying with lots of alcohol. I thought this was a bit strange, considering the alcohol problems his dad had when Ricky was younger, as well as how that contradicted much of what they taught Ricky about success in school and church values. Then again, they were 750 miles away from Ricky, who was now getting used to the concept of discovering he had the freedom to make these decisions all by himself. Ricky discovered the more he partied, the less he was treated like he had a target on his back, so he continued to party when his second floor friends invited him along. He also discovered it helped numb the pain he felt inside, regarding all those years of abuse and pressure to succeed in school. After all, everyone is friends with everyone else as long as there's plenty of alcoholic beverages to go around, even if you're a complete nerd like Ricky!

One Sunday morning that changed for Ricky. After a night of not drinking, he was awakened at around 7:30 am by someone lightly grabbing his shoulder, after which he heard an audible voice clearly tell him, "something in your life needs to change". When he looked up there was no one else in the room with him. Half asleep, his first thought was that this was yet another prank "fos" and his abusive friends were doing to torment Ricky, making him think he was hearing voices. Because he was alone that morning, Ricky's first instinct was to check under his bed, his roommate's bed, behind both desks, and pretty much everywhere else he figured his roommate would have hidden a portable audio device to make him think he was hearing voices. He was still groggy and didn't give any thought to the mysterious hand grabbing his shoulder, just what the voice said to him. After searching for about half an hour, he remembered that since it was a Sunday morning, "fos" and friends were likely passed out at some party off campus. Ricky liked to drink, but he rarely drank to the point where he passed out at a party without being brought home by his misfit friends.

After coming to this realization, Ricky sat on his bed and thought about this strange advice from this unknown voice for another half hour. His epiphany was that the thing he needed to change was to start attending church again every Sunday. So he got up, showered, got dressed, ate breakfast at the campus cafeteria (a Sunday morning rarity among the drinking crowd), then went to the Sunday chapel service at the campus chapel. As he continued in his rediscovered faith relationship, he realized that this was exactly the something that mysterious voice told Ricky was what he needed to change about his life.

The more he went, the more motivated he was to make the necessary changes in his life to become the person his parents thought he was supposed to become. One way he expressed his newfound faith was to write Bible verses in colored markers on his white sneakers. He still had no real motivation or guidance on how to improve or what the person he wanted to be looked like, but he was heading in the right direction, or so I thought.

That decision took an unexpected turn for the better when he met his first crush, named Karol, in early February. Most of the students who had the ability to talk to and develop relationships with members of the opposite sex went to what was considered the college equivalent of the prom that night. Ricky and a few of his misfit friends instead went to the alternative event for those who lacked the social skills to find that special someone to attend the formal prom event with. Now as far as having the experience with dating and females, Ricky still had nothing to rely on. So when he met Karol for the first time that evening, he didn't really know how to act around her, but in spite of how clueless he was beneath the surface when it came to understanding women, he tried his best to appear mature around her. His restored faith certainly helped. Karol was a strong Christian, which Ricky sort of was as well, having grown up in the church. They got along well and enjoyed spending time together on campus for the rest of their freshman year. When they separated for the summer, she went on a mission trip to Mexico, while Ricky went home to work seventy-five hours per week, as a groundskeeper at a country club during the day where his dad's best friend was the head groundskeeper, and as a full-service gas station attendant in the evenings and on Saturdays. Since state law prohibits customers from pumping their own gas in New Jersey, all gas stations must have an employee pump gas for customers.

When he did have some free time, Ricky spent it with his neighborhood friend Carlo. Their favorite activity was spending time at the nearby harness racetrack, where Carlo taught Ricky how to bet on horses. Ricky's mom prayed Ricky would lose the first time he went so as not to get addicted. This was probably the only time in Ricky's life where his mom ever openly shared with Ricky that she prayed on his behalf. Unfortunately, those prayers were not answered as Ricky hit the daily triple that day, which for the uninformed horse gambling enthusiast, is correctly picking the race winner in three consecutive races. For Ricky that meant a $140 payout on a $2 bet. After that, Ricky made sure that anytime he went he would leave his credit cards in the car, while only putting between $25-30 in his wallet, to ensure that was the extent of the money he lost, if he lost on any given day. That way, he still had a fun time enjoying the races themselves without any of the stress of losing more than he wanted to lose.

When there was down time at the gas station, which was quite often, Ricky wrote handwritten letters to Karol every other week. It normally took two weeks for Karol to reply to Ricky's letters from down in Mexico. Today the idea of a handwritten letter sounds strange, given the internet and how much easier it is to communicate, but back in 1990, handwritten letters were still the primary means of long-distance communication. To Ricky, each letter from Karol not only helped him begin the process of understanding how to relate to a woman that wasn't his mother, but it also helped him find a basis with which to develop a stronger Christian faith. Another good perk of working that many hours that summer was knowing he was rarely ever home, and as long as he worked those long work weeks, he didn't have to deal with any more long, painful conversations with his parents. Because his evening job involved sitting around waiting for customers, when he wasn't pumping gas, he used all that free time to write Karol, relaxing and unwinding after a hard day spent maintaining the golf course grounds. Since he and his neighborhood friend Carlo developed a much closer friendship after high school, thanks to their mutual hobby of going to the racetrack, Carlo often came by to chat and hang out with Ricky at the gas station. Since the station was on the western corner of the triangle in the center of town, it wasn't a long walk there or back for Carlo.

When they got back to school for their sophomore year, Ricky moved down to the second floor to be around his true friends. While the abuse finally stopped, his relationship with Karol slowly grew distant. Ricky thought it had a lot to do with his immaturity, because let's face it, he certainly had no skills when it came to understanding how to relate to women. He had never been intimate with anyone, nor had he ever been on an actual date, so he didn't know what the right way to act around a woman was. All the misfit friends he bonded with were equally clueless when it came to understanding how to relate to women. So when the relationship with Karol finally ended a few months later, Ricky's emotional life completely fell apart. Looking for someone to blame, he blamed Jesus Christ for all the pain and suffering he went through for the past fourteen years of his life. Like so many others, Ricky concluded that a God who loved him wouldn't allow him to experience this much neglect from his parents, along with all the pain, abuse and rejection from friends, females, and fellow students, culminating in this sudden rejection from his first true crush. So he completely pushed all semblances of Christianity out of his life, and wanted nothing to do with faith anymore. The only remaining emotion he did leave for the God he grew up around in church was one of hatred – the same hatred he felt towards all his classmates who abused him mercilessly. I was hurt by Ricky's decision. I really wanted him to continue to rely on his faith in Jesus, given the depth of the pain he felt after his relationship with Karol fell apart. In the aftermath of this decision to walk away from his faith, he travelled down a dark road, a five-month period full of frequent thoughts of suicide, culminating in a decision to make the effort to do so. His plan was to take all of his unused medications, put them all in one bottle, and just take them all at once. This five-month journey of emptiness culminated in this one decision, the decision whether to end or not to end his life, unsure of what waited for him on the other side. All he could rely on was the feeling that his life no longer had meaning or purpose, and no bright prospects for this promising future his parents always deceived him into believing he was capable of. Even his choice for a major – computer science – was leading to failure. He was often able to successfully work out the program codes on paper, but when it came to programming them into a computer, he was only successful with the very first program assignment from his first class. As for the reasons why his programs never worked, he often stumped all of his professors, including the department chairperson, leading them all to also give up trying to help Ricky after considerable effort.

But in the meantime, he still had to please his parents by continuing to appear to do well in school. He was persuaded by a next door neighbor to take a sports officiating class, figuring it would be an easy A for Ricky, to help boost his grades. He certainly didn't have the self-confidence to be successful doing something as high-stress as officiating sports, but he did get the easy A for the class. Shortly after completing the class, he was thrown into working an intramural volleyball match all by himself. The instructor was supposed to be there to mentor and guide Ricky to begin the process of learning how to officiate successfully. But she never showed up, leaving Ricky alone to officiate by himself. There, he got his first taste of being yelled and screamed at by twelve angry females, all of whom were upset that Ricky made maybe one or two calls all match. As he stood up there on the platform sweating bullets, the only thing he wanted to do was finish the match and leave. Making matters worse was the fact that "fos" happened to be the only fan in the stands. He did survive the match, even lasting the whole match without quitting. From what I later heard from Ricky, he said the match would have gone better with no referee.

During this dark night in his soul, there were only three good things that happened for Ricky. The first good part of this dark period in his soul was losing his desire to masturbate, as he didn't even find value in it while trying to decide whether he should live or die. The second good thing to come from this darkness came about after he was eventually talked out of suicide by another next door neighbor at the time, a fellow misfit named Derek. Derek used his leadership skills as a political science major to bring Ricky out of his depression in an unexpected way. It may not have been the best option to lead Ricky away from suicide, but it was the only option at the time. So when the third good thing to come from this suicide attempt, becoming a part of a group that could help lead him out of his suicidal funk, he reluctantly went along for the ride, a ride that helped him navigate the storms that would soon follow. His adventures with this new group of friends is the subject of the next chapter.

10

Riders on the Storm

> *"Riders on the storm*
> *Into this world we're born*
> *Into this world we're thrown*
> *Like a dog without a bone, an actor out on loan*
> *Riders on the storm"*
>
> "Riders on the Storm", The Doors

For the first two months of the calendar year, during the first half of spring semester, attending social events to receive free food and gifts is a common recruiting tool used by fraternities and sororities to ensure the continued survival of their respective organizations. With his newfound friends from the second floor going to numerous events for the free stuff, Ricky simply went along with the fellow misfits he now called friends. It didn't matter that he drank heavily every weekend to fit in. All he wanted was the ability to be in an environment where he was around people who somehow managed to find value in him as a person, not as a means to justify his abusers' self-worth. The idea of meeting fellow heavy drinkers in a non-alcoholic social setting with the chance to get free stuff was one all his new friends enjoyed. So when these friends decided they were all going to pledge a fraternity, they invited Ricky along for the ride. The fact that his grades didn't meet school standards to allow him to legally join didn't matter to anyone involved, Ricky included. They were willing to take Ricky in anyway, as they all knew it was probably his best chance to find a way out of the suicidal crater he called life, and help him discover that his life had hope and meaning. Their acceptance of him also let him know that he was now around people who had his back, regardless of how socially dysfunctional he was, even with his suicidal tendencies. Being in an Animal House type fraternity (with Ricky being an almost identical version of the Larry Kroger character from the movie) where everyone was a misfit made for an unusually strong bond between them. Like the characters in the movie this fraternity had physics geeks, gigolo types who were good with the ladies, life of the party types, heavy metal guitar player types, a skateboarder, rednecks, future politicians, a dancer, the biggest pessimist you have ever met, a wannabe gangsta murderer type (not Ricky), an overweight philosopher who liked to walk around the frat house in his underwear, a big redneck who stole anything that wasn't bolted down, and a few other undesirables like Ricky who, based on their current social status, had little chance of a successful social life outside of the fraternity. In spite of all their differences, the only things they had in common were heavy alcohol drinking, a desire to do anything to piss off the bureaucratic college administration, and the willingness to stand up for each other.

As to whether or not the school knew about Ricky's acceptance as a pledge with the fraternity is something was Ricky was never informed of. He did continue to attend counseling throughout his fraternity adventure, though he always thought his counselor was a complete idiot who overgeneralized using generic psychological concepts as a cure all solution. What I mean is that this counselor only had one solution to each problem and applied the same solution to all his clients, rather than taking the time to get to know each person individually and apply a unique solution based on each person's unique personality differences. As a result, Ricky never much cared for the guy, but went anyway just to check the box about having continued to see the counselor in the aftermath of his time spent contemplating suicide.

Now there was some concern from the actives as to whether or not Ricky would be able to handle the rigors of pledging without snapping or giving up, but they weren't willing to bend their standard to let him in. The school might have but they didn't. When it came time to decide on a pledge class leader, the rest of the class agreed that Derek was the best fit.

As pledging began, Ricky and the other eleven pledges spent most of their free time working on their homework (which for Ricky was not very often). Each pledge class had to come up with a name and slogan for their pledge class. Ricky and his pledge mates chose the title of the chapter as their group name, based on the song by the rock group The Doors. It was a fitting tribute to the unique challenges the pledges were presented with overcoming. One such challenge was working together to complete a monstrously large, five-thousand piece puzzle chosen by the actives. Unfortunately for their class, the puzzle they had to complete had no distinguishing landmarks that made completing it easier. The entire puzzle consisted of various types of flowers growing in an open field. In some ways, working on the puzzle was more mentally draining than the evening pledge activities. Ricky put in most of the work, as he often found it to be a way to destress from the real world, since he was never criticized or pestered by the actives while working on it in the frat house. Ricky most liked the idea of being left to work in peace when he did, and he liked his alone time trying to challenge his mind, in ways that keeping up with his classes didn't do for him. He still lived to barely squeak by with his grades, as his only genuine motivation was still avoiding his parents' wrath and disappointment by failing to live up to their lofty expectations for his bright future. Ricky also learned the fraternity symbol was the mythological bird known as the phoenix. The phoenix represented the fraternity's inability to die. Instead of dying, it would return to the fire it came from, as an allegorical representation of the purification fire used to overcome adversity. For Ricky, even though he spent his whole life attending church, this was the first time he was given the opportunity to discover spiritual concepts such as rebirth and overcoming fires of adversity.

As for the evening "activities", they involved at least an hour in the frat house basement with the pledges having to put their noses against a black concrete wall, pledge paddle in hand, while being yelled at by the actives. They were expected to answer questions about the fraternity itself, or its members to avoid a form of punishment often involving the pledge paddle. Now that modern culture totally devalues physical pain as being abusive, I will leave how the paddles were used to the reader's imagination. His parents used the wooden spoon to the same body part, with the only drawback being that it hurt to sit down in a chair for a few hours afterwards. Unlike Ricky's mom, the actives obeyed the unwritten rule of not being allowed to "break wrist". That meant when using the paddle the wrist had to remain straight to lessen the force of the paddle. Ricky was very familiar with that disciplinary based, military lifestyle, having grown up in that type of environment at home. The only difference was that his parents always broke wrist, since their goal was inflicting as much pain as they could to bring home their militaristic message. Not breaking wrist meant much less pain, so for that reason the punishment didn't bother Ricky, or the other pledges (and if it did they weren't allowed to speak up), because they were expected to be strong enough to handle it.

Now before I continue with Ricky's story, I wish to state that things like this happen in fraternities and sororities all across the country. Hazing laws have become much stricter, due to problems arising from the personality attributes of the people in charge of running the activities. When they lack maturity, compassion, limits, or restraint, like the Chapter 1 version of Ricky, the situations can easily get out of control. Thankfully, the active fraternity members did treat the pledges in such a way as to demonstrate compassion and concern for their overall well-being. The rule about not breaking wrist is an excellent example. Having said that, the point of this discussion is NOT intended to reveal the secrets of the fraternity pledge process, to open the door for additional discussion on what is or is not considered hazing, nor is it to give lawmakers and college administrators a reason to waste money on yet another witch hunt for anything remotely resembling hazing. The pledging process Ricky went through was very beneficial to his future.

His pursuit of completing the pledge process, with people he knew finally cared about him as a person, gave him a reason to rediscover the value of life. For that, I know Ricky would have been forever grateful.

Occasionally the pledges did get to do fun things, with one pledge event offering two choices: going on a scavenger hunt for random items around campus, or trying to steal the holy grail of the fraternity: a big ceramic / metal hog outside some redneck's store about twenty minutes from campus. Since it had been stolen numerous times by previous pledge classes, the store owner had that hog bolted down so heavily, with so much lighting, the pledges would have had an easier time successfully robbing a bank. So they chose the scavenger hunt option.

There were many other memories, with two Ricky recounted in detail. The first was the night his pledgemaster got wind of Ricky's decision to divulge to a female he knew at lunch in the cafeteria, that he was pledging illegally. His mistake was doing so in the presence of the overweight philosopher, who was also pledging with him. As the rest of the pledges were bonding over stories while working on the puzzle, Ricky was called into a one-on-one session with the pledgemaster in his room – who by the way was the dancer of the group. Because of his passion for dancing, he knew all the dancer exercises. He was called in right after Derek, the pledge leader, who likely was also punished for something he did wrong. When Derek left, Ricky entered to face his punishment. This was Ricky's first – and only – introduction to what a dancer situp was. Forty-five minutes later, he temporarily had abs of steel – and the intense pain and redness that goes along with such an intense core strengthening exercise. In spite of the pain, he was willing to endure it for the sake of his pledge brothers, and the bond they all had with each other, whether good or bad. Helping him endure the pain was largely made possible by his belief that his friends had his back, now he had to step up and fight to ensure he didn't lose that lifeline to his friends.

The second event Ricky recounted was the final night of pledging, known as hell night. They had to wait in their dorm to get the call to show up at the fraternity house. When they got the call, the bells began ringing from across campus (which was a loop of the intro to Hell's Bells by AC/DC). With the huge speakers set up in the fraternity house front lawn, they were loud enough to be heard clear across campus. As the bells rang on that cold, dreary, death-filled Friday night in the heart of that black Michigan winter – BONG ... BONG ... BONG – all the pledges came running as a group to the frat house to begin hell night. After more nose time with the black concrete wall, along with some other special methods used to test each pledge's trust, all the pledges were blindfolded, and taken to sand dunes along Lake Michigan. Once there, their first challenge was to climb one of the dunes, carrying a toboggan loaded with necessary supplies such as hand shovels, bottles of drinking water for the pledges, and other necessary items. With around a sixty-degree incline and a distance of between one-third to one-half of a mile to the top, climbing the dune was a big challenge. Though he wasn't big, Ricky had the cardio endurance to easily make it, but it was a challenge even for him. That forty-five minute session doing dancer sit-ups helped him a lot. For some of the bigger members, like the overweight philosopher, their poor cardio endurance meant they needed help getting up to the top. Those that could make it also had the added burden of taking turns pulling those that couldn't continue the climb up, using the toboggan. When they all got to the top, in spite of the challenge, the first instruction the pledges got from the actives was to dig an individual trench for themselves using the hand shovels, which symbolically represented dying to self. When the pledges were almost done with their trenches, some active members took all the pledges for a distraction exercise, while the rest of the actives stayed back and filled in the holes. When they came back they had to repeat the process of digging a trench a second time. When they were about done, they were taken away for another distraction exercise. The holes were then filled in again. The third time they were told to dig one big pit for all twelve pledges, which they reluctantly did, hoping this time their hole wouldn't be filled in again. Thankfully, it wasn't. The point of creating one big hole was to remind all the pledges to live and die as a group of brothers. Once they were done, they all had to lie down on their backs, feet touching in the center of the giant circular trench. Thankfully, no one was literally buried. But they did grasp the point of the exercise as explained by the actives as they lay in the circular trench, that being dying to self for the good of your brothers.

Once pledging was over, they learned the secret handshake, and other important rules for members, which I won't discuss, as I never officially joined their fraternity. After that was done, some stayed up and had a few drinks followed by the usual run to Denny's for 3:00 am night munchies, but the vast majority called it an early night due to the physical exhaustion that followed hell night. The next day there was a graduation party between the fraternity and their sister sorority. There Ricky met his second crush Nikki for the first time. Nikki pledged that year as well, but she was a freshman. Ricky liked her because she had a beautiful face and aura of kindness about her. He liked slim women, but not ones that seemed to be high maintenance. He also liked what he saw from her as far as how she carried herself – her presence around people, if you will. She didn't share the same interest in dating Ricky, which was true for many other women. I'm sure she knew what most others knew – that he was clueless when it came to women, had no idea how to treat them, looked mostly at their appearance, and still masturbated regularly to help him deal with his own insecurities. Now Nikki had a boyfriend at the time, which meant Ricky would have to wait for her breakup. He may have hated Jesus, but he still had some of the moral values he grew up with, just without the religious parts. Joining the fraternity helped restore his faith. This time around, however, alcohol was now the deity Ricky had faith in, and parties were his new weekly church service. Ricky even got to be the music director at every "church service", with his CD collection earning him the role of DJ at all their off-campus parties.

Shortly after joining the fraternity, his sophomore year was drawing to a close. Since computer science was no longer a viable option for him, Ricky needed to change majors, as his final opportunity to change majors was at the end of his sophomore year. With a little guidance from his fraternity brothers, he chose Business Administration as his fallback degree option. He chose this because a few of his fraternity brothers were also pursuing that degree, and also because his liberal arts curriculum put him in a position where it was the easiest major to switch to from computer science. He had already taken a few of the introductory classes for a Business Administration degree, making it somewhat of a no-brainer decision. His new major brought on new advisors, with the same level of career guidance he'd gotten from every other adult influence in his life – little to none.

When he returned for his junior year, Ricky did "date" someone other than Nikki. She was a short, pudgy redhead who pledged a different sorority than Nikki. She also happened to live next door to Nikki that year. Ricky wasn't attracted to her at all. He only "dated" her because he thought that if he dated someone that lived close to Nikki, she would share stories about how cool Ricky was, thus leading Nikki to find Ricky attractive. He assumed women liked to talk about stuff like that, which is the only reason he pursued this relationship with the pudgy redhead. At first Ricky's fake "girlfriend" was fun to be around, but as time wore on she got more physically and verbally abusive with Ricky, so he broke off the relationship. He never admitted he was only using her to get closer to Nikki, not even to his fraternity brothers, hoping maybe that when the opportunity presented itself, he could get a chance to date Nikki on the strength of the success of his relationship with the pudgy redhead. That long awaited breakup between Nikki and her boyfriend did happen about eighteen months later, though obviously Ricky hadn't matured at all during that time. As much as he had hoped, Nikki never had any interest in Ricky. He was still the same idiot he always was, only now he had alcohol and mischievous fraternity brothers to guide him in his journey, minus the Christian faith he grew up with back in New Jersey. Suicide, and the aftermath of blaming Jesus for his past, had eliminated any desire to further his faith relationship anymore. In its place was birthed a hatred for all things religious / spiritual. That especially included Karol, whom he now avoided completely any time he saw her around campus. Whenever Ricky saw Karol approaching, he'd cross the street long before she got within eye contact, so as not to have to look at her or talk to her.

In the meantime, a few months after her breakup Nikki began dating a new boyfriend, a guy she'd eventually end up marrying. Her new boyfriend always hated having Ricky around, as I'm sure she must have told him about Ricky and his interest in dating her. In spite of this, Ricky often hung out with her and her sorority sisters as they were still cool people he had an ok relationship with, they just never saw him as anything more than the immature idiot he was back then. Honestly, based on what I knew about the person Ricky was at that time, I don't blame them one bit.

The last two years of college were ok for Ricky, with the help of his new brothers. He moved into the fraternity house for his last two years of college, but they weren't allowed to drink on campus. Instead, as with most other fraternities and sororities, each had their own specific party house, and each one had a special nickname it was known by. Ricky's fraternity party house was one half of a duplex known as Wasteland, and it was the most popular party house among current students for two reasons. One, they had two members who worked at the local party store, where they could purchase the kegs of alcohol at the cheapest prices. Two, they passed on those savings to the partygoers, rather than use part of the money to pay the monthly rent. As a result, the house would easily be standing room only every time there was a party there. Once they even had the leader of a local gang show up to one of their parties, but when he and his associates were asked to leave, on their way out they slashed the tires of the 1989 Mustang convertible owned by the top ladies' man within the fraternity.

Two hundred plus attendees was typical, which made their parties the most attended off-campus party house. Because of the low prices buying kegs of alcohol, they kept the entry fee at $1. Other party houses would charge $5 or more to attend a party, using the difference towards helping cover the rent for the house. That wasn't usually the case at Wasteland. Any college student knows a $1 entry fee is better than $5 or more! Even when they raised the entry fee to $2 per party, they still grossed enough to cover all expenses. As I mentioned earlier, Ricky got to play the role of DJ. Since he enjoyed music, he quickly developed the biggest CD collection among the group, and everyone enjoyed his skills as DJ. Most attendees were drunk, so what he played didn't really matter as long as they had something to dance to while they drank. He continued to party heavily every weekend, most of which was done after the party was winding down, because he had to maintain his bearing playing the music. When it came to partying, he was always successful at it. However, when it came to his pursuit of Nikki, he was never successful. While he continued to wait for his opportunity to date Nikki, he at least had a reason to enjoy life along the way, around brothers he could count on to look out for him, even when drunk.

After four years of college Ricky was still twelve credits shy of graduating, so he stayed for a fifth year of college as a part-time student, but marched with the class he arrived with. Due to his failures in computer science, his pursuit of the next logical degree option, coupled with his limited motivation to succeed in life in the aftermath of his suicidal ideations, Ricky earned the honor of being what he often called the "anti-salutatorian" of his graduating class. If valedictorian is the top graduate and salutatorian is second, anti-salutatorian meat Ricky was second from the bottom. That he graduated at all was itself an accomplishment. But his parents were there, beaming with pride seeing Ricky with his graduation gown on, honoring the family name by being the first member of the family to graduate college, even if he was extremely unmotivated, as most anti-salutatorians are.

To Ricky, the college degree and the ensuing six figure executive job was still his parents' dream for his life, not his own. In spite of the degree, he still had no clue what he wanted to do with his life. A Business Administration degree doesn't create open doors for success unless it comes with a vision and a drive for success. Thanks to the lack of mentorship and guidance from the adult influences in school and at home, Ricky was still years away from having the knowledge, wisdom, and maturity to understand what that vision and drive consisted of. The only thing further away than that, was having a vision and drive for success he could call his own. So with his hand holding that piece of paper that was so important to his parents, and his mind and heart holding nothing except for a motivation to party, drink and seek pleasure wherever he could find it, it was now time for Ricky to enter the real world – a world he clearly wasn't prepared for.

11

Youth Gone Wild

> *"Since I was born, they couldn't hold me down*
> *I'm another misfit kid, from another burned out town*
> *I never played by the rules, and I never really cared*
> *My nasty reputation takes me everywhere ...*
> *They call us problem child, we spend our lives on trial*
> *We walk an endless mile, we are the youth gone wild"*
>
> *"Youth Gone Wild"*, Skid Row

Most people who earn the honor of being the anti-salutatorian or anti-valedictorian of their class, move back in with their parents for free rent, since they usually have a difficult time finding a good job. Ricky, on the other hand, broke tradition, since he considered his fraternity brothers his closest family at the time, primarily because they were the only ones who ever listened to him and encouraged him to be the person he truly wanted to be – himself! So naturally, he wanted to continue to mature through their friendships. It was better than going back to the world he grew up in, living with parents who would continue to nag him endlessly to be the successful person they wanted him to be. It was an obvious choice, or at least it seemed the better choice to Ricky. Ricky heard about an off-campus party house from a fraternity brother, not far from campus. He agreed to move in there while he earned the final twelve credits he needed to officially graduate.

The title of the chapter, based on the song listed above, also happened to be the song Ricky considered his theme song at the time. He even wrote the chorus to the song (the last two lines quoted above) around the wrist of every pair of work gloves he wore, to remind him that it was possible to rise above all the times he was abused or neglected, although all that pain led to him developing a motivation to rise above based on tearing others down out of revenge, not building them up.

Because of this motivation, along with his poor grades, Ricky wasn't given too many opportunities for success after college. He recounted one particular interview he had with a rental car agency recruiter shortly after college. Now this recruiter was straight to the point and spoke his mind with no filter. When he saw Ricky for the first time, wearing a mismatched suit, he knew that Ricky's clothing choice made a poor first impression, and was willing to tell him as such, in a constructive manner, of course. Because Ricky had just graduated, he didn't have the money for a new suit, nor did he have the guidance from anyone to lead him to believe that buying a new suit – one with coat and pants that actually matched – was something important to have. When the administration's only focus was suicide prevention, career guidance isn't part of the rehabilitation protocol. A suit wasn't something his blue-collar parents ever had to wear, so Ricky never grasped its' importance. Based on this, and a few other interviews, not surprisingly, Ricky completed his first summer after college without finding a decent paying job to support himself.

The closest he came to discovering a career he could sort of call his own, involved a decision to one day work towards becoming an owner or executive of a professional sports franchise. Given his dad's passion for sports, coupled with his inability to please his dad by making it as a player, and his newly acquired Business Administration degree, that was how he figured he'd make it in his life, so as to fulfill his parents' dream for his successful future.

His career started with a job at the local parks and recreation department. With his vast experience officiating (that one volleyball match I mentioned earlier), he was terrified at the prospect of wanting to endure that type of abuse again, so officiating wasn't an option Ricky wanted to pursue. Instead he started out keeping score for games, as well as cleaning out the local arena, which at the time was the site for all of Ricky's college basketball team's games, both men's and women's basketball. These were jobs any high school kid could have done, but Ricky saw them as a starting point for a future in professional sports. In his mind this was the first step in paying his dues climbing the ladder of success to the top of the mountain of owning / managing a professional sports franchise. He also used his free time to study lots and lots of sports statistics, such as who won the Super Bowl every year, who that year's regular season and Super Bowl MVP were, and so on for all four major professional sports.

Meanwhile, rent in his five-bedroom dump was only $115 for the small room he called his own, so he didn't need to make a lot of money to pay the rent. All the other expenses, however – food, alcohol, car insurance – were a struggle for Ricky. Since Ricky wasn't making enough to cover those bills with what little work he was doing, and was never taught about the concept of fiscal accountability, he turned to credit cards to help him cover the difference. It took him a few months to discover the dangers of doing that without being able to pay them back in a timely manner, but given his attitude towards life, and how little things like credit card debt meant to Ricky's outlook on life at the time, he didn't really care. He was having fun, enjoying life with people who liked to drink and party. That was all that mattered to Ricky.

His landlord at the time, Kevin, was a few years older than Ricky. He shared a similar hedonist lifestyle, having developed it through being a member of another fraternity on campus. After having agreed to move in there, Ricky met many of Kevin's friends and the other roommates during his time there. Like Wasteland, this house also had a nickname that students knew it by – Looney Tunes. It wasn't much of a party house, but occasionally a few students came by and hung out. Most of the parties involved Kevin's closest friends. Evenings were usually spent on the porch listening to a police scanner one of Kevin's friends brought by. Once they got the scanner working, everyone sat around chatting over cases of beer, while being entertained by the local crime events that happened to be going on that evening. Since the neighborhood on the other side of 16th St. housed Mexican families that worked at one of three nearby furniture factories, there was a Mexican gang presence there. Most of the college students were also aware of this fact, so only the brave partygoers crossed over to the other side of 16th St. to drink. Ricky never thought it was that bad. None of the Mexican families ever saw Kevin's crew as a threat so they left them alone, and Kevin's crew did the same with the Mexican folks living around them. In the winter, not much happened due to the brutal Michigan winters, since they did get all the lake effect snow coming off the lake. Everyone always knew when spring rolled around when they heard their first gunshots. Two incidents stood out. The first happened the night a man ran towards Ricky's house, stopped at the house directly across the street, fired two to three gunshots at the house, then continued running up the hill, away from the house he fired at. The other involved a small gang tussle around the corner from Looney Tunes. A fight broke out, and police / ambulance were called to deal with a man who'd been shot with buckshot pellets (ball bearings) fired from a twelve-gauge shotgun. Kevin's crew occasionally heard about all sorts of other events on the police scanner, and if it was close enough to Looney Tunes, so long as it wasn't dangerous and the police were already there, occasionally they'd swing by to check out what happened too. Welcome to la vida loca!

After Ricky officially completed the last twelve credits in order to officially graduate, Kevin's brother Mike moved in for the summer, having planned to spend the summer bonding with Kevin. Having Mike around was the best thing that could have happened to Ricky. They quickly developed a strong friendship, spending a lot of time together. They shared a passion for Beavis and Butt-Head episodes, Ultimate Fighting Championships, disc golf, playing backgammon almost every day, and of course, lots of alcohol drinking. They even got hired to fill two positions taking turns collecting fees for a township boat launch that summer, as the township decided to collect fees for residents and non-residents to launch boats for the first time, to help pay for some new township projects. Not many residents were pleased by the decision, but Ricky and Mike were just there to collect a paycheck, even if it wasn't all that much. Coupled with his job working for the recreation department, which now also included umpiring little league baseball, Ricky was actually making enough money to pay for rent and bills, without having to use his credit card. Mind you, he still used his credit card for the important expenses like alcohol and social activities. Now even though he had a friend he could be himself around, the darker side of himself also slowly began seeping out, as evidenced by the influences described in Chapter 1 that slowly led Ricky down his dark, dismal quest for revenge.

As for Mike, he met a girl named Melissa that summer and they started dating. They were also sexually intimate, which at the time didn't matter much to Ricky, as he didn't really care about dating, as trying to stay afloat financially was difficult enough. He knew his ship with Nikki had long since sailed, and he was ok with that. As he began his own pursuit of the hedonist lifestyle, he began to realize that things would never work out between he and Nikki anyway. He was also ok with the three musketeers type relationship he had with Mike and Melissa. As their three-musketeer relationship developed, they discovered they all shared a common bond over baseball, with Ricky being a Yankees fan, and Mike and Melissa were both Tigers fans, with former Tiger catcher Mickey Tettleton being Melissa's dream man. Because of the closeness of their friendship, Melissa once bought Ricky a plastic New York Yankees helmet as a souvenir gift. At the time, Ricky valued it because compared to all the other gifts he'd received, this was the first time in his life he'd been given a gift that truly felt like a gift from the heart, with no strings attached. For reasons I will mention later, this gift would have a much deeper influence in Ricky's life.

In the meantime, at the boat launch job, their responsibility was to document the number of day and seasonal passes sold to both residents and non-residents. Non-resident passes were a little more expensive than resident passes. Since Ricky had no moral compass at the time, he took many of the non-resident seasonal passes he sold and marked them as resident passes so he could pocket the $10 difference. He did the same thing with some of the day passes, pocketing the $2 difference. Since this was about the time he was slowly becoming the version of Ricky I wrote about in Chapter 1, in large part because of his secret hatred for all things moral or religious, he didn't see anything wrong with skimming money to support himself. Knowing he could get away with it, since he was left to his own (non-existent) capacity for honesty when filling out his reports, made it a guilt-free decision. As long as he turned in most of the money he collected, it was ok for him to skim money from his job.

After the summer job ended, and Mike went back to school to finish his degree, Ricky discovered a local bar / restaurant called JJ's. Ricky went there not only for a social life, but also because they had this new trivia game that appealed to Ricky's thirst for knowledge. In spite of his limited funds for drinking, he became a welcome addition amongst all the regular trivia players. One night per week they featured a sports trivia game. Since Ricky wanted a career in sports administration, playing this weekly sports trivia game provided Ricky a strong motivation to continue his studies of all things sports, to challenge his knowledge of sports-related questions. With the help of two other sports buffs, they always finished with really high scores. The highest was the week when Ricky finished second nationally in individual rankings, earning himself a phone call from the corporate office to inform him he won a camping tent as a prize for his second-place finish. While the tent was advertised as a "three-person tent", Ricky barely fit in it while sleeping diagonally, and he was only 5'11" tall. So Ricky eventually donated it to a local Boy Scout troop.

Career wise, Ricky moved on to a job working for a hot dog joint with an owner who was the type of person Ricky's dad would have been if he had owned a restaurant. The owner happened to be Nikki's next-door neighbor when Nikki was a child. Ricky therefore assumed he must have been a nice person like Nikki. Ricky instead discovered, even with his broken moral compass, that this owner was a complete jerk with an irritating micro-management mindset. It totally contrasted the personality he imagined a next-door neighbor of Nikki should have. Particularly irritating was the demeaning, verbally belligerent treatment the owner dished out on his employees, not just Ricky. It made stealing hotdogs to feed his fellow housemates something he thought was just compensation for the poor treatment. They were the good quality, one lb. beef hotdogs, not the cheap stuff you'd find in a store. Ricky also hated the owner for being promised an assistant manager position, only to have him go back on his word and give the job to a nineteen-year-old female with no college education.

One day Ricky was left hanging by another co-worker and had to close the store all by himself. It normally took one hour for two people to clean up and close the store. With Ricky being left to close the store alone, one would naturally think that it would take one person two hours to close it. I should mention here, that even though Ricky didn't have any moral integrity, he was always a clean freak, and made sure to do a good job cleaning. After all, his dad's mantra of "do the job right the first time so you won't have to do it over and over again" stuck out in his mind like a recurring nightmare, and even Ricky knew the health and safety issues with not thoroughly cleaning a store that sells food.

Unfortunately, he was more intelligent than his owner in this area, as the owner called him the next day to ask him two questions. First, he asked him what time the store closed. Surprisingly, Ricky answered honestly, more so because he had to make sure his story was the same as what the store hours were. The next question Ricky was asked was what time he left. Here he also answered honestly in accordance with when he punched out two hours after closing. The owner then told him he was fired and hung up. Ricky put the cordless phone down, told his roommates what happened, then went back to watching TV as if nothing was wrong. While his roommates discussed the merits of how unprofessional it was to fire someone over the phone, Ricky didn't much care to join the debate. He felt like someone who had just found out his prison sentence was about to be commuted, with an unconditional release to occur that day. The only downside, in Ricky's mind, was that he wasn't able to steal food to feed himself or his roommates anymore.

As for the house Ricky lived in, most of Ricky's roommates were slobs who likely had never been taught what a scrubber sponge, mop, and/or a broom were. When one roommate moved out, each new replacement was more of a slob. It got so bad that the porch was eventually stocked with dozens of full trash bags that never got taken out. It was so foul smelling, no one went into the porch due to the stench of the trash. The dishes never got washed either. Well everyone's but Ricky's. Ricky still had that militaristic upbringing, and the haunting reminders to act responsibly ringing in his ears like tinnitus. In keeping with his militaristic upbringing, Ricky's dishes got washed daily, though in order to keep them that way, he realized it was in his best interest to lock his dishes in his room, taking them out only when he wanted to cook, then cleaning them and securing them back in his room after he was done. That was the only way he could ensure they would be clean anytime he wanted to use them.

As this lifestyle continued for the next few months, knowing that Kevin wasn't doing anything about it, Ricky's recurring nightmare mantra from his dad brought out the worst in Ricky. It was here that Ricky had his Private Pyle moment, deciding to flood the kitchen sink to send that message. Doing so also meant flooding the entire kitchen floor. Ricky thought it needed a good cleaning as well. The flooding continued into the walkway down to the basement, where Kevin's room was. When the slobs started coming home three to four hours later, they knew Ricky was responsible, but they weren't willing to go up there and confront Ricky. The noose on his door served as a reminder that confronting Ricky could be risky. In spite of his Private Pyle mindset, it was Kevin's responsibility as the landlord to confront Ricky, and their argument in Ricky's room was quite heated. At the end of the conversation, Ricky handed Kevin the knife, demanding he kill him. Kevin refused, instead throwing the knife at Ricky's box fan, chipping an edge of one of the fan blades before storming out of the room. For Ricky, this became just another mind game he gradually developed an increased interest in playing. After his incident with Kevin, it took him hours to calm himself down enough before he could even consider leaving his room, not only for fear of what his roommates might think of Ricky's actions, but also because of how Ricky might have reacted while his psychotic, Private Pyle mindset still raged inside him. As he pondered what he did, thoughts of chaos, anger and hatred flooded both his mind and his soul, and he enjoyed those thoughts. Like Private Pyle, it was all a result of the long-standing anger he had for everyone who abused him, as well as his hatred of Jesus for putting him through all his abuse. Since these feelings were never ones Ricky could express and work through constructively growing up, they ended up manifesting themselves in psychotic outbursts like this one. As I mentioned earlier, his counselors only addressed the issue of suicide, instead of finding out about Ricky and addressing the deeper issues involving all the abuse, to help him constructively deal with overcoming his pain in a way that was specific to his personality.

In spite of his chaotic mindset, he did still volunteer for a local Boy Scout troop in town once a week. Morally, he certainly wasn't a good role model for the kids, as he allowed the scouts to bring out his rebellious side, but only in ways that were not so over-the-top as to draw the ire of the other leaders, like when he bought Dharum cigarettes for the Scoutmaster's son and his best friend, both of whom were only fourteen at the time. The same was true for any high school or college age students who were under the legal drinking age. If they came by Looney Tunes, Ricky was more than willing to buy alcohol for them. All he cared about was that they paid well for his services. Again, while he was raised with a moral conscience at home, in church, and in the Boy Scouts, now that he was free from the oppressive tyranny that he associated with those three aspects of his life, along with the hatred he had for both Jesus and the abusers he was forced to call classmates in school, he simply stopped caring whether or not what he did affected others positively or negatively anymore. Financial survival became his only external motivation.

Graduating college meant Ricky was finally free from most of the people and the beliefs that insisted he become who others wanted him to become. With his degree, he could now become his own person, even if that meant gradually deteriorating into someone who desired to trample over others to achieve success. He didn't care who he had to step on or manipulate to succeed, nor did he care if anyone wanted to be a part of his passion for getting revenge towards those that made his life hell in school. It led him to openly view anyone lacking his superior intellectual capacity as a "f$&%ing loser" not worth his time.

Even his career focus as a successful executive of a professional sports team, deteriorated into nothing more than a desire to use his future riches, influence, and power to manipulate others like marionettes. In this game, Ricky was the only puppet master, desiring vast riches as a tool to manipulatively pull the strings of all his employees. His desire for success became heavily tainted with all those negative influences that I discussed in Chapter 1. Instead of looking to make everyone else proud of him, all those influences led Ricky to see career success as a means to both fulfill all the self-serving dreams his parents pushed him to succeed in, and to fulfill his own desire to avenge himself against everyone that made school a living hell for Ricky. This hybrid, cryptic, morbidly psychotic form of success motivated by a desire to take advantage of his employees as an act of selfish, greedy revenge against all his classmates slowly morphed into his only goal in life. His only motivation for doing so became looking out for number one, leading him to view everyone else as unworthy of his intellectual superiority. There was even a time in his life when Ricky claimed he was more important than I was.

But then Mike left to finish his college degree, and it was time I did what I needed to do to rein in the psychotic monster that Ricky was quickly becoming. I knew Ricky remembered who I was, since he'd already read the book I authored twice, cover to cover. Now that I was back in his life, it was time I took rightful control. You see, I AM more than just an ordinary friend to Ricky. I happen to be The Creator and Sustainer of the universe, God in three Persons: Father, Son and Holy Spirit. As the true Narrator of Ricky's life, I began the process of ending Ricky's life, spiritually speaking that is. I had to utilize My supernatural power over Ricky, as natural influences simply weren't going to break through to the psychopath he was becoming. As for how I accomplished this, I'll let Ricky take over as narrator and tell you himself.

Thanks God. As the author of this book, Ricky isn't just a fictional character I made up. The character of Ricky in this story is me, and this is the true testimony of my life. Now I'm about to finish this book by explaining how God spiritually ended my life to this point, like He just mentioned, in granting me an entirely new life rooted in His will for my life. Sorry if it's not the physical death you were anticipating. The spiritual is more profound than the physical anyway. As you'll find out in the final chapter, it was a spiritual fight I – in my downward psychotic spiral, motivated by my pride-filled state of anger, revenge and hatred for all things spiritual – was determined to win, even considering how my adversary was the God of the universe. The battle lines were drawn, and the war was about to begin.

12

... on the road to Damascus

"I had a come to Jesus revelation
In a blinding light I saw my soul's salvation
My feet don't falter, my limbs don't ache
Through the waterless land of the thorns and the snake
I could taste the freedom in the back of my throat
My burdens too heavy for me to tote
So I fell to my knees I dug a hole down deep
Dropped 'em in a bottomless pit for the Devil to keep"

"Damascus Road", John Mellencamp

Now I've heard claims by people who think my story is pure fantasy, based on events that never really happened, or like my parents claimed, that I really wasn't that bad of a person. You're welcome to ask those that knew me either during my time in the fraternity, or during my time at Looney Tunes, how much potential I displayed for one day unleashing an unstable, psychotic explosion. There are three people in particular you can ask, and this chapter is devoted to explaining their role in my conversion. Specifically, I deal with how they influenced my willingness to allow God – and when I say God I refer to one or all three of the members of the God-Head Trinity: Father, Son and/or Holy Spirit – to begin the process of changing my heart, mind, soul and especially my spirit. They did so through a series of supernatural, divinely inspired, soul crushing encounters.

The first encounter came during a Boy Scout event. At the event, I happened to be talking to one of the Scouts – he was known to everyone in the troop as "Stinky". In our discussion, I learned that Stinky was a busboy at the same Bob Evans' restaurant that Melissa happened to work as a server. Out of curiosity, I happened to ask him what he thought of her. His only response, typical for a hormonal teenager, was to answer, "she's hot". As his response hit my brain waves, I was completely overwhelmed with an unfamiliar passion for Melissa, at least that's the best way my finite mind can accurately describe what I experienced. The intensity of the experience was unlike anything I'd ever experienced at any moment in my life to that point. It was much greater than anything I felt towards Karol or Nikki. The problem came when I realized I was still the same immature, clueless idiot I'd always been when it came to relating to women. I was also still steeped in my own fantasy world of masturbation, which only made it more challenging for me to understand this passion. The non-existent education I received from my parents regarding sexuality further complicated my ability to understand it. My role as social abusee left me with little understanding of constructive inter-personal relationships. In spite of these many shortcomings, I was expected to figure out what this totally unfamiliar passion was. I had never been taught anything about passion in any aspect of life (unless you count my passion for revenge or hatred of Jesus), or how to go about understanding it. Given the super-genius stigma my parents instilled in me since I learned to read, my hatred for Jesus led me to seek to learn how to love others through all those famous philosophers I wrote about in Chapter 1. Instead of giving me the answers I sought, their "wisdom" contributed heavily to my quickly developing psychotic mental state. The more information I absorbed from these renowned secular thinkers, the greater my foolish, ignorant, stubborn pride became. Growing at an equal rate was my bloodthirsty desire for revenge against all my abusers. It was here that my pride manifested itself into thinking I was more important than God Himself. For obvious reasons, He was about to show me just how wrong I was to think that.

My second encounter with the supernatural was hearing God speak to me inside my heart and mind. In order to rein in the depth of my pride, and to begin the process of teaching me how to change from continuing to become the drunken angry monster that I often saw my dad become during my first ten years of life, God asked me to agree to a covenant. The terms of this covenant He was asking me to agree to, was this: I was to agree to help ensure the salvation of the three people that I was closest to at the time — my landlord Kevin, his brother Mike, and Melissa. As for why God would make such a request of me, at the time, I didn't have a clue. I also didn't know why God chose these three people, but even an emotional idiot like me could figure out why he included Melissa, more so after this intense, yet unfamiliar, passion for her remained inside of me. I knew about the somewhat familiar spiritual rule I had learned, that being when God wants to do something profound, He does it in threes. Spiritually, that was the only plausible explanation I've ever been able to come up with as to why God would include all three of them in this covenant, instead of just Melissa. Because of the proud psychopath I was becoming, I simply blew God off. I thought to myself, what right does God have to dictate to me how, when or why I should bind myself to some stupid covenant? Who does God think He is?

Now those questions meant I was anything but eagerly willing to go along with what God was asking of me. I still hated Jesus with every part of my being. I still blamed Him for having allowed me to endure all the abuse I lived through the first fourteen years of school, for the thoughts of suicide, for not giving me any knowledge how to relate to women, for my failure to please my parents through athletic pursuits, for my failure to live up to their dream for my career success in life, for not being able to develop a mentorship bond with either parent, for being taught next to nothing by my parents in the way of real world lessons I needed as an adult, and most of all, for all the emotional wounds that were reopened anytime someone ridiculed me for any of the deficiencies in my life. To me, all of that was Jesus' fault, so my initial response was screw you God, I'll figure it out on my own (though my choice of words was a lot less civil).

In response, God began speaking to my soul, reminding me many times that no matter how much of an analytical super-genius I perceived I was, God frequently reminded me that I knew nothing about how to love. Each new reminder only made me even more angry and more determined to prove, in my idiotic pride, that God was wrong and that I did know how to love others. The result was a more intense desire to pursue my study of secular philosophers and psychologists, thinking they held the answers I needed in order to discover how to love someone, without turning to this Jesus that I despised. In my efforts to prove God wrong, there were two actions I decided to take. The first was when I chose to anonymously write some inspiring letters to close to fifteen hundred or so students on campus, using the moniker of White Lightning. The white represented purity, and the lightning represented the ability to strike quickly and without warning. To avoid detection, I even glued my fingers so that my fingerprints wouldn't appear on any of the letters I sent to my fellow college students. Problem was, writing the six letters may have been inspirational, but they weren't something I really believed myself. I just wrote them to prove to God how wrong He was. This was little more than a naïve attempt to convince God I knew what it meant to love, but He never bought it. I doubt many others bought it either.

The second action I took was the Saturday after Thanksgiving that year. I decided to go to a party by myself solely with the intent of making love to some random female stranger. I found a small party nearby, and began scoping out women. There weren't many to choose from as not many women were around during the holiday weekend. Now some people might be surprised that I managed to make it all the way through college without ever having sex, but most everyone who knew anything at all about me in both high school and college, would verify just how clueless I was when it came to knowing anything about how to relate to women. A good example was the time I took a trip to party in Chicago with some fraternity brothers. When partying there, I bet the brother who told me about Looney Tunes, that I could pick up a female at a bar that night. This fraternity brother took my bet, knowing it was an easy win for him. I still remember the name of the place – Bongo Johnny's Dance Shack – and they offered .10 drafts with an $8 cover charge. Well I spent about ten bucks on alcohol that night, only to lose the bet to this fraternity brother, proving how clueless I was around women. At college, most female students also knew I withdrew into my own imaginary, fantasy world of masturbation to fulfill my sexual fantasies. It was still a lot less risky than being hurt or exposed for my testicular / relational / emotional deficiencies. I also struggled with confidence / maturity issues around women as a result.

This was never more evident the one time I hung out with just Melissa. I couldn't really call it a date, since we were kind of just friends at the time. I didn't really know where she stood with Mike, and didn't know how to bring up the subject. We went to Red Lobster for dinner and went to the beach after that. It was a cold November night so we couldn't go down to the water, which Melissa enjoyed. Instead we sat there chatting in my car, where it became obvious that I had no clue what to say to her. As our time ended, I gave her a lame peck on the cheek. Looking back, I came across as romantic as a dead fish that had just washed up on the beach. She probably knew it too – who wouldn't? I certainly didn't have the history of knowing anything about dating relationships to that point. Because of my masturbation addiction, my entire desire for a mate was based solely on their bodily appearance. In that spirit, I remember once asking Melissa if she was a cheerleader in high school, since in my ignorant, vapid, shallow naïvete, cheerleaders were the only type of people whom I considered physically worthy of dating. Most of the time I "dated" the pudgy redhead, I relied on alcohol to provide me the inspiration to continue to date someone I was only ever using to get to Nikki.

So at this Thanksgiving weekend lame party, I was going to find a woman to make love to, in order to prove God wrong. With a condom in my back pocket and a second one in my wallet, I was, as a Bud Light commercial once claimed, "up for anything". I didn't care who she was, or how she looked. My only goal was to lose my virginity that night, in order to prove that I knew how to love a woman. As the night wore on and the drinks kept flowing at this lame party, I did meet an ugly freshman, and I won't mention her name so as not to embarrass her. Normally, I wouldn't have given her a second thought, because while sober I thought she was ugly, plus she was a freshman and I was a fifth year senior. Since I was up for anything, and the drinks were flowing, this night was different. We got to know each other a little, and established a physical and emotional connection. This connection led us back to her dorm, well after curfew hours. As we entered her dorm, I started to get passionate, and things began to get even heavier once we got to her room. Being prepared for such an occasion, I pulled out the primary condom out of my back pocket. As I tried to unroll it, it broke due to the heat from it having been in my back pocket for the past few hours. Fortunately, I had a backup in my wallet. Unfortunately, it also broke due to the heat when I tried to unroll it. Thinking this was the end of my efforts, she let me know that she was on the pill so it would be ok. In my drunken stupor I figured I'd take her at her word, so I began taking my pants off. As I got them down to my ankles, which was a challenge considering how drunk I was, I saw a bright light coming from outside her window. Stunned, I looked outside to see what the light was. Outside her third floor dorm window, at 3:30 am I locked eyes with an angel, arms crossed in displeasure and a stern look of disgust on its face. What really terrified me was when I stared into the face of this angelic being, I found myself momentarily staring at Nikki's face. Even stranger was the fact that this was the exact same room Nikki lived in three years earlier, her freshman year. For the Bible fanatics, the fact that I was in room 316 was possibly a reference to the famous verse in the book of John, but that certainly didn't mean anything to me at that moment. This angelic being didn't have to say anything, the look of disgust on its' face said it all. In that moment I found myself instantly sober with a big 'ole dose of terror coursing through my blood. Without saying another word to her, I quickly pulled up my pants and sprinted the ten or so blocks it took to get home. I ran as fast as my legs allowed, without ever bothering to look both ways for traffic. Then again, there wasn't any vehicle traffic at 3:30 am on a holiday weekend, since most students went home to celebrate with family. Even though it was a college town, it was still a conservative Dutch Reformed Christian town. Had I been timed for my running speed that night, I'd probably have been selected for the US National Track and Field team representing our country at the Olympics. Perhaps I could have beat Usain Bolt in his prime, but I guess we'll never know for sure. After all I was considered the fastest kid in the 'hood, so it might have been possible! When I did get home, I was extremely winded and short of breath. Kevin and another roommate or two were still awake at that late hour, and naturally they wondered why I was so out of breath and what happened. Even if I could breathe normally and give them a response, I had no clue how to explain what just happened. I certainly didn't know how to convince anyone else I'd just seen a pissed off angel, when I didn't fully believe it myself. Now I understand the possibility that in my drunken stupor I was merely imagining seeing something outside her window. Rest assured, this was no product of my drunkenness or my imagination.

The next day everyone was especially curious to know about my exploits from the previous night. I mentioned the girl's name, as I did still remember that much, but other than that, I just mentioned all the details prior to seeing the Nikki angel outside her third floor window. I had to somehow save face without actually discussing that part of my experience, or the fact that we never had sex due to the angelic intervention. Letting everyone else decide for themselves what happened turned out to be my best-case scenario. Trying to convince unbelievers of a supernatural, divine intervention is almost impossible, especially when I myself didn't fully believe it was possible. Though we joked about my supposed sexual exploits with this female for weeks, pronouncing her name in French as if to make her sound more appealing, I never did tell anyone the truth of what happened that night – until now. But God's involvement doesn't end there.

Because of the haunting reminder of this incident, my fear of even attempting to date women while sober, and the regular reminders from God about how I didn't know anything about love, there was a New Year's Eve party at JJ's a month later, with a buffet and unlimited champagne for $25.00. Because I was a trivia regular, having gotten to know many other regulars there, I decided to pay the fee to attend. The longer I stayed there, the more depressed I got. Each time I saw couples getting intimate with each other only served to remind me that I was alone because God was right to state that I knew nothing about how to love people. In response I became more and more of a booze hound, sucking down as much champagne as I could to block out the pain of being there alone, having to watch everyone else there enjoy intimate moments with their significant other. The more I drank, the less I thought about the fact that the three members of the Trinity were right. So while everyone else had a great time celebrating the start of the new year with their loved ones, each time I allowed myself to consider the possibility that God was right, I had an emotional breakdown. Fortunately, I was able to hold it in until I made it to the bathroom stall, where I could break down into tears without anyone noticing. I had three of those breakdowns that night, at least while I was still sober enough to remember them.

Later that winter, I was back at JJ's playing trivia with my regular friends a few months later, and happened to run into Melissa there hanging out with some of her college friends. When she saw me, she gave me a real special hug that meant so much to me. It was totally full of compassion and kindness for herself and others, a feeling I rarely ever experienced to that point in my life. I still remember that interaction quite well, but never truly knew how to tell her that, given my clueless capacity to relate to women. That was a memorable experience, considering this passion for Melissa that still lived inside of me, though I was still no closer to understanding it.

The more I thought about that encounter, with this unfamiliar passion still inside of me, the more I began to realize that Melissa is that once in a lifetime soul mate you just know is destined to be the one you happily spend your life with. But there was still this issue of my inner spiritual war against the God of the universe that I was heavily engaged in, and stubbornly determined to win.

Later that year, in early spring, this spiritual war of attrition brought on the next challenge. I returned home from work like usual, to the trash dump that I called home. As I walked through the front door, I suddenly felt a pair of hands grab me from behind, in between each side of my shoulder and my neck. Because of where it was grabbing me, and the force of its' grip, I wasn't able to turn around and look to see who (or what) was doing this. Before I even had a chance to look at my shoulders, I found myself being pushed to the ground, face down. The pressure continued until I was lying on my stomach in the middle of the living room floor, unable to do anything to resist whatever now had me pinned to the floor. Once I was securely face down on the living room floor, I found myself spiritually taken to a place of complete darkness. Since my body was still lying face down on the floor when my roommates all came home later that afternoon, according to what they later told me, I can accurately conclude that this was an out of body experience. My eyes were opened in this "place", and I was able to see clearly, only there was nothing to see. A few moments later, I could feel the presence of many strange beings with me in this place. I also knew exactly what they were thinking. There could have been dozens or perhaps even thousands of them, I don't know. I couldn't see so I wasn't able to count, but that wasn't why I was there. The only thing I could discern in this place was the thoughts of all these beings slowly closing in on me from all sides. All of them were so depraved in their thoughts, all they thought about was tearing me apart with their claw like fingernails. How they could see me I don't know, but they were obviously more attuned to this place of complete darkness than I was. Terrified, I cried out from the depths of my soul to get me out of this place. I didn't even know who to cry out to, I just knew it wasn't going to be Jesus. I had to plead with someone – anyone – to get me out of wherever I was at that moment. Since I'd read my Bible twice already, I remembered reading II Peter 3:17, which speaks of a place of blackest darkness. The only possible conclusion I could draw from that verse, was that I was just given a glimpse of what the part of hell that consists of blackest darkness was like. After begging to be brought back to where my body was, I was brought back to my prone body, still lying face down on the living room floor. How long I was there, I don't know. As I just mentioned, many of my roommates saw me lying on the floor unconscious when they came home. Even though it was around 4 pm in the afternoon, they either assumed I fell asleep or that I was drunk. As with the angel, this wasn't an experience I could fully believe myself, let alone know how to explain it to someone else without them thinking I was insane. So for the second time, I said nothing about what actually happened.

I'd also like to say I gave in and agreed to what God was asking of me. I did at first, but eventually my hatred of Jesus was far stronger and more influential than anything else inside my heart and mind. While the reality of God's covenant request of me was in everyone's best interests, it didn't take me very long to change my mind and reject God yet again by going right back to gorging myself on all those secular philosophers for guidance. His pursuit continued.

Two months later, the next conflict in this war occurred when God again showed up on the morning of April 19, 1995. For those that know their history, that was the first time America experienced a large-scale terrorist attack by American citizens. The event in question was the Oklahoma City bombing, which I mentioned at the end of Chapter 1. While everyone else saw the horror associated with all those lives lost, I was largely indifferent to what was going on. This time God came right out and confronted me directly, much like that rental car company's hiring representative. I recall the conversation going like this:

> God: "Do the actions of the people responsible for the bombing remind you of anyone?"
>
> Me: "No, should they?
>
> God: Yes.
>
> Me: Who?
>
> God: You.

Spiritually, God just drilled me right in the head with a baseball bat the size of a fully grown tree, and a lot harder than I could have ever done to shark and his shiver. It wasn't until I stared at the palms of my hands shortly after that brief conversation, that I recognized the depth of my hatred and the anger I saw in my hands at that moment. Deep down I knew God was right on point with his conclusion in comparing me to McVeigh and Nichols. I was staring right into two entirely wicked hands capable of doing something exactly like what they just did in Oklahoma City, or possibly worse. Now instead of accepting God's realistic conclusion and agreeing to the covenant He was asking of me, I still stubbornly believed there had to be something good inside of me without God. Entertaining that thought led me right back to the same philosophy books that had now become a large part of my identity. I believed so fervently that there had to be some innate goodness inside of me without Jesus. The only real reason was because I still allowed my hatred for Jesus to have a greater influence in my life, more than any other emotion inside of me. I even include this growing unfamiliar passion I now had towards Melissa in that list as well. As a result, I was totally led by depravity, wickedly bound, and obstinately determined to rely on secular philosophy as a replacement for Jesus, through which I could find all the answers I needed in life. I should have simply accepted the futility of my eternally stupid decisions and trusted His ways as being higher than mine (Isaiah 55:8). But I didn't. I still wanted complete freedom from the oppressive religion of this man named Jesus that I grew up learning about, still blaming Him as being the source of all my suffering.

Shortly after that, I once broke down in tears at the spiritual conflict from living with both this unfamiliar passion for Melissa and my hatred for all things spiritual, and when asked why, I tearfully admitted my interest in dating Melissa to Kevin and Mike. Melissa even told me around that time how she looked great in a skirt. Given how physically attractive she was, I believed her, though I never got a chance to find out. But they both tried to set me up to date her. However, my tears weren't based on my interest in her. My tears came anytime I reminded myself of the painfully obvious realization God kept telling me: apart from Him I had nothing good inside of me to offer someone so kind-hearted and special as Melissa, only a wicked side that would have physically hurt her terribly bad had we dated. My tears also came from realizing the futility of trying to find some good in me apart from Jesus. Looking at my hands after the OKC bombing left me with the realization that God was correct in his assessment that I was quickly becoming a psychotic monster. The sobering realization of just how badly my wicked hands would have hurt Melissa if we did date, was the most painful truth I had to live with, considering this passion inside of me towards Melissa, and it spiritually wounded me deeply. Because of what God was calling me to do, those tears were also a result of this being the first time I began to understand the source of this passion for Melissa inside of me. I still had a long way to go to truly understand it, but I realized that the source of this passion had its root in none other than Jesus Christ Himself, the very same Jesus I completely despised. That realization also meant this passion could only be fully, truly understood by surrendering my life to Jesus, agreeing to this sacrificial request of God the Father, Jesus Christ the Son, and Holy Spirit, for the eternal benefit of Kevin, Mike and especially Melissa. So when I cried those tears, the most important reason I cried was because I also knew it meant having to turn down the opportunity to date her at the time, so as to answer God's call for my life. The agony of knowing I only possessed a capacity to badly hurt someone so kind, so sweet, so caring, and so truly special was the deepest source of my tears at that time.

So I again agreed to go along with God's covenant regarding the salvation of these three people. But eventually, my mind got involved again. Yes, my super-intelligent, manipulative game-playing, abuse-avenging, infinitely proud, Jesus-hating mind took control yet again, leading me back to the same secular philosophers for guidance on how to figure out everything entirely on my own, without the Jesus that the core of my identity still believed to be the source of all my pain and suffering. So I eventually changed my mind, and rejected His calling for my life a third time.

God then turned up the spiritual pressure another notch. After choosing to get lost spiritually travelling my own road (leading to darkness) yet again, God chose to walk alongside me. Everywhere I went, I could sense His presence watching me. It was a hyped-up version of what is commonly known as a sixth sense, when you know someone is within five feet of you in your personal space. You can't see them, and you don't want them to get that close to you, but you know they're there, and that unsettling awareness that they are there causes you to abruptly stop what you're doing and react by finding out what they want. When they're there, you ask them what they want in such a way as to strongly convince them to go away and leave you alone to do whatever it was you were doing before the interruption. With people, they usually get the hint and go away. However, when it's the God of the universe who has total control over everything that exists, if He chooses to remain in your personal space for as long as He wants to, there's really nothing that can be done about it. If He did choose to speak, which was rare, he always asked the same nagging question: Would you sacrifice your future here on earth to agree to this covenant to help ensure the salvation of these three people? (This was very similar to the way my parents would nag me with their question of, "When are you going to get a real job?" every time we spoke.) At first my answer was always an intense, "hell no, screw you God, I can figure out how to love entirely on my own", but the more I discovered how special Melissa was, not only physically but also with every bit of her kind personality, and the more intense this passion for her grew inside of me, the deeper I thought about the question each successive time God asked me. Not only was I wondering why I would be asked such a question multiple times, but it also got me thinking what purpose was there to answering yes to such a strange question directly from God. Again, I've always been given this super-genius stigma, so I might as well live up to it. After all, if God is all-knowing, He already knows how and when to plant the right seeds in someone's heart and mind, even in the case of someone who was the pride filled, super-genius, Jesus-hating, manipulative mind-game playing, psychotic monster that I was quickly becoming.

The best answer I could come up with through my finite attempts to analyze and dissect the nature of the question, was that He wanted to help me understand what it meant to sacrifice my own best interests for the good of someone else. Like I learned during fraternity hell night, I was expected live out the lesson I learned then, in sacrificially dying for a brother (or sister, in Melissa's case). The one thing I wasn't going to do was allow Jesus to have anything to do with either the question or the answer to the question. I still saw myself as this highly skilled, manipulative mind game player who needed to guard his mind and heart from any further emotional pain inflicted on me by this Jesus, and oh yeah, did I mention I still hated Jesus?

The longer God stalked me, the more I realized I was now the one being played mind games with by the God of the universe. That only intensified my hatred of Jesus more, because I still thought in my over-inflated sense of superior intelligent pride, that I was the only one who could play mind-games with people and win. I didn't even care to acknowledge the fact that my adversary in this war of intellectual attrition was the omnipotent, omnipresent, omniscient God of the universe, the God of Abraham, Isaac and Jacob. So for a time, I simply ignored God, doing my best to pretend He wasn't there in my personal space watching everything I did. Every time He asked me that stupid question about sacrifice, I simply ignored the question. But each time He asked, I slowly warmed up to the idea of answering yes to the question, because I began to envision how much more beautiful of a person Melissa would be if she lived for Jesus. But I couldn't openly answer yes to the question, as my passionate hatred for Jesus was still far stronger than any other emotion I felt, including this passion for Melissa. To this point in my life, I always had the mental strength to win every other battle of intellectual attrition, successfully keeping everyone out of my heart, courtesy of the impenetrable wall that was my supposedly superior mind. For that reason, I figured if I ignored God's spiritually overbearing presence long enough, He would eventually get the hint and leave me alone. Boy was I wrong!

That realization flattened me like a freight train would the day I happened to want to get some milk out of the refrigerator. I sauntered down the stairs towards the kitchen fridge to grab the gallon jug. At first, I didn't notice Mike and Melissa making out by the kitchen sink, the same sink I recently flooded. My only focus was getting a drink of milk. However, as I looked up and noticed them there with the kitchen window as a backdrop, Melissa slowly turned to look at me. I suddenly found myself in what I can best describe as what you feel when you watch a super slow-motion replay on TV. When our eyes connected, time seemed to come to a complete stop as I stared into her eyes in that terrifying moment of infinity. I don't honestly know what it was I was looking at through her eyes, but I do know with absolute certainty that what I was seeing was an infinite vastness of purity that extended infinitely out into the horizon. This vision totally flooded every possible sensation I'd ever experienced, and this sensation was a million times more overwhelming than that day I first experienced that passion for Melissa after my conversation with Stinky.

At that moment, to say I was totally terrified to the innermost core of my being would be a huge understatement. I quickly pushed the door to the fridge away from me to close it, then sprinted back upstairs to my room, the same way I did after I had to inform the drunken dad monster to come join us for dinner. In my terror, I didn't want to be noticed or have to look at anyone else on my way back upstairs. As with the angel incident, I wasn't about to stick around the kitchen any longer than I had to. In my terror, I may even have taken the entire milk container with me, since putting it back meant risking the possibility of being seen by either Mike or Melissa. Being anywhere near them, or anyone else at that moment, was completely out of the question.

When I finally made it back to my room all I could do was cry out in complete surrender. I found myself totally emptied, knowing every single ounce of pride and self-sufficiency came completely crashing down in the aftermath of that instantaneous, terrifying moment of infinity. I simply couldn't handle another second spent fighting God. The experience so broke me of every last worldly attachment that I clung to for support up to that moment, to this day the memory of what I saw through Melissa's eyes in that moment makes looking people directly in the eyes a major struggle. Now I know that most psychologists posit that not looking people in the eye is a sign of low-self esteem. Trust me, I've read my share of secular psychologists as well as secular philosophers. Given this unusual, specific experience, low self-esteem is not the case with me, but I know most people only look at the obvious psychological explanation on the surface instead of digging deeper. Rather than try to explain why my situation is different, I simply let people think what they want. It is a lot easier than explaining the deeper spiritual reasons why I struggle to look people in the eyes, since most people don't grasp spiritual matters anymore.

Now my decision to surrender completely to His will meant acknowledging that I would be permanently agreeing to His eternal, heavenly, covenant promise to help [Jesus] ensure the salvation of these three special people. I also knew this was the end of the line regarding my relationship with Jesus. Either I was going to continue to allow my hatred of Him to get the best of me and eventually face the eternal consequences of doing so, or I was going to completely surrender and permanently go along with His plans for my life. God made that decision abundantly clear after this breakdown, when He told me in no uncertain terms that if I refused to follow Him this time, there was not going to be another opportunity to do so. I pondered the ramifications of the decision, with my mind and my heart FINALLY working together in unison. Granted, most every thought and feeling I had in those moments were based on an absolute terror of what else might God do if I permanently rejected his will for my life. It was as if God was finally choosing to answer my wisdom of Solomon prayer from six or so years earlier, which is in line with what one of the writers of Psalms wrote: "The fear of the LORD is the beginning of wisdom; all who follow his precepts have good understanding. To him belongs eternal praise." (Psalm 111:10, NIV) So I put all the pieces together of everything I had experienced the past seven or so months, both with regards to the temporal (earthly) and the eternal ramifications of my decision. All my thoughts came back to the terror I believed I would have to face, had I refused to accept my final opportunity to accept His will for my life. I also kept going back to that question I'd been asked over and over by God, "would you sacrifice your future pursuits here on earth to help ensure the salvation of these three people?" With mind and heart finally working together, I realized that the answer to this and every other question was a resounding: Yes, Lord, I'll do what it is You are calling me to do, in spite of how painful the road might be from here on out. I surrender, I'm Yours now, use me as You wish. But I do have one favor to ask in return. Since You are asking me to sacrifice my career pursuits for the sake of this covenant, to help ensure these three people will spend eternity with You, would You grant me a second chance to date Melissa when You think I'm ready to date her? She deserves my absolute best, and You correctly informed me that without You there is nothing good inside of me worthy of her, so I can accurately conclude that right now I have nothing worthwhile to offer her. I did learn in Sunday School that if I trust you, and ask anything according in accordance with Your will, you will hear my prayer and grant me my petition. Since agreeing to God's covenant meant living to do His will, I was shocked to hear God say yes to my request for a second chance to date Melissa! I just didn't know when that would happen, but I had to learn to trust God that He would be faithful to His promise to make it happen in His time ... someday. In the meantime, I had no idea what to expect from this point on, but I knew it would involve many trials to test my faith. Now if you think the story ends here, think again – this journey with Jesus has only just begun for me! And so the story continues ...

> "I will give you a new heart and put a new spirit in you;
> I will remove from you your heart of stone and give
> you a heart of flesh." (Ezekiel 36:26, NIV)

About the Author

Thank you for reading my story detailing the divine influence regarding the profound ways I became a true follower of Yeshua H'Mashiach. Though this is only my first book, I hope you'll also want to read the rest of the story, as told in the other two books in this Damascus Road Trilogy. My story has led me to a passionate desire to share how suffering can lead to positive life change that provides eternal meaning and purpose. I plan to do this by focusing on spiritual truths everyone needs to understand, which is especially important considering the unfortunate, growing presence of dichotomous, cessationist beliefs present within many of today's Christian churches. Along with my cat Hobbes, I split my time living in both Grand Rapids, Michigan and Oak Grove, Kentucky, but my sacrificial desire to serve the spiritual and financial needs of my fellow military servicemembers, as both a Religious Affairs NCO in the Army Reserves, trained Family Readiness Liaison, President/CEO of the Referee Association of Military Servicemembers, and President/CEO of Modern Day Paul Ministries, takes me all over the world.

Printed in the USA
CPSIA information can be obtained
at www.ICGtesting.com
JSHW020729271023
50722JS00001B/36